GRAPHIC ORGANIZERS
AND OTHER
VISUAL STRATEGIES

ENGAGE THE
BRAIN

MARCIA L. TATE

CORWIN PRESS
Classroom

For information:

CORWIN PRESS

Corwin Press
A SAGE Publications Company
2455 Teller Road
Thousand Oaks, California 91320
CorwinPress.com

SAGE Publications, Ltd.
1 Oliver's Yard
55 City Road
London EC1Y 1SP
United Kingdom

SAGE Publications India Pvt. Ltd.
B 1/I 1 Mohan Cooperative
Industrial Area
Mathura Road, New Delhi
India 110 044

SAGE Publications Asia-Pacific Pvt. Ltd.
33 Pekin Street #02-01
Far East Square
Singapore 048763

Printed in the United States of America.

ISBN 978-1-4129-5225-5

This book is printed on acid-free paper.

08 09 10 11 12 10 9 8 7 6 5 4 3 2 1

Executive Editor: Kathleen Hex
Managing Developmental Editor: Christine Hood
Editorial Assistant: Anne O'Dell
Developmental Writer: Jeanine Manfro
Developmental Editor: Colleen Kessler
Proofreader: Bette Darwin
Art Director: Anthony D. Paular
Cover Designer: Monique Hahn
Interior Production Artist: Karine Hovsepian
Illustrator: Jane Yamada
Design Consultant: PUMPKiN PIE Design

GRADE **1**

TABLE OF CONTENTS

Connections to Standards

This chart shows the national academic standards that are covered in each chapter.

MATHEMATICS	Standards are covered on pages
Numbers and Operations 1, 2, 3	9
Algebra 1, 2	9
Algebra 3, 4	11
Measurement 1, 2	21
Data Analysis and Probability 1	9, 17
Data Analysis and Probability 3	15, 17
Problem Solving 1	9, 11
Problem Solving 2	23
Problem Solving 3	19
Problem Solving 4	23
Reasoning and Proof 1	9
Reasoning and Proof 2	11
Communication 1	9, 13
Communication 2	9
Communication 4	15, 17, 19, 26
Connections 1	9
Connections 2	15, 17
Representation 1	9, 15, 17, 23
Representation 2	19
Representation 3	13, 15, 17

SCIENCE	Standards are covered on pages
Science as Inquiry 1, 2	32, 38, 40
Physical Science 1	40
Physical Science 3	38
Life Science 1	27, 30, 32, 34, 37
Life Science 2	27, 32, 34

978-1-4129-5225-5

Life Science 3	32, 34, 37
Earth and Space Science 1	38
Earth and Space Science 2, 3	44
Science in Personal and Social Perspectives 1	82
Science in Personal and Social Perspectives 4	38

SOCIAL STUDIES	Standards are covered on pages
Social Studies 1	47, 53, 54
Social Studies 2	46
Social Studies 3	46, 53, 57, 59, 63
Social Studies 4	54
Social Studies 5	50, 53, 54, 59
Social Studies 6	57
Social Studies 7	50, 59
Social Studies 8	46
Social Studies 9	50, 59
Social Studies 10	57

LANGUAGE ARTS	Standards are covered on pages
Language Arts 1	65, 67
Language Arts 2	74
Language Arts 3	65, 67
Language Arts 4	76, 79, 81
Language Arts 5	67, 76
Language Arts 6	71, 79, 80
Language Arts 7	76, 78
Language Arts 8	78, 81
Language Arts 9	72, 78
Language Arts 11	76, 78, 81
Language Arts 12	67, 69, 71, 72, 81

Introduction

An ancient Chinese proverb claims: "Tell me, I forget. Show me, I remember. Involve me, I understand." This timeless saying insinuates what all educators should know: Unless students are involved and actively engaged in learning, true learning rarely occurs.

The latest brain research reveals that both the right and left hemispheres of the brain should be engaged in the learning process. This is important because the hemispheres talk to one another over the corpus callosum, the structure that connects them. No strategies are better designed for this purpose than graphic organizers and visuals. Both of these strategies engage students' visual modality. More information goes into the brain visually than through any other modality. Therefore, it makes sense to take advantage of students' visual strengths to reinforce and make sense of learning.

How to Use This Book

The activities in this book cover the content areas and are designed using strategies that actively engage the brain. They are presented in the way the brain learns best, to make sure students get the most out of each lesson: focus activity, modeling, guided practice, check for understanding, independent practice, and closing. Go through each step to ensure that students will be fully engaged in the concept being taught and understand its purpose and meaning.

Each step-by-step activity provides one or more visual tools students can use to make important connections between related concepts, structure their thinking, organize ideas logically, and reinforce learning. Graphic organizers and visuals include: idea web, KWL chart, Venn diagram, number line, bar graph, T-chart, maps, chain of events map, magazine pictures, photos, color chart, magnetic letters, glyph, word wall, feelings chart, and more!

These brain-compatible activities are sure to engage and motivate every student's brain in your classroom! Watch your students change from passive to active learners as they process visual concepts into learning that is not only fun, but also remembered for a lifetime.

Put It Into Practice

L ecture and repetitive worksheets have long been the traditional way of delivering knowledge and reinforcing learning. While some higher-achieving students may engage in this type of learning, educators now know that actively engaging students' brains is not a luxury, but a necessity if students are truly to acquire and retain content, not only for tests, but for life.

The 1990s were dubbed the Decade of the Brain, because millions of dollars were spent on brain research. Educators today should know more about how students learn than ever before. Learning style theories that call for student engagement have been proposed for decades, as evidenced by research such as Howard Gardner's theory of multiple intelligences (1983), Bernice McCarthy's 4MAT Model (1990), and VAKT (visual, auditory, kinesthetic, tactile) learning styles theories.

I have identified 20 strategies that, according to brain research and learning style theory, appear to correlate with the way the brain learns best. I have observed hundreds of teachers—regular education, special education, and gifted. Regardless of the classification or grade level of the students, exemplary teachers consistently use these 20 strategies to deliver memorable classroom instruction and help their students understand and retain vast amounts of content.

These 20 brain-based instructional strategies include the following:

1. Brainstorming and Discussion

2. Drawing and Artwork

3. Field Trips

4. Games

5. Graphic Organizers, Semantic Maps, and Word Webs

6. Humor

7. Manipulatives, Experiments, Labs, and Models

8. Metaphors, Analogies, and Similes

9. Mnemonic Devices

10. Movement

11. Music, Rhythm, Rhyme, and Rap

12. Project-based and Problem-based Instruction

13. Reciprocal Teaching and Cooperative Learning

14. Role Plays, Drama, Pantomimes, Charades

15. Storytelling

16. Technology

17. Visualization and Guided Imagery

18. Visuals

19. Work Study and Apprenticeships

20. Writing and Journals

This book features Strategy 5: Graphic Organizers, Semantic Maps, and Word Webs, and Strategy 18: Visuals. Both of these strategies focus on integrating the visual and verbal elements of learning. Picture thinking, visual thinking, and visual/spatial learning is the phenomenon of thinking through visual processing. Since 90% of the brain's sensory input comes from visual sources, it stands to reason that the most powerful influence on learners' behavior is concrete, visual images. (Jensen, 1994) In addition, linking verbal and visual images increases students' ability to store and retrieve information. (Ogle, 2000)

Graphic organizers are visual representations of linear ideas that benefit both left and right hemispheres of the brain. They assist us in making sense of information, enable us to search for patterns, and provide an organized tool for making important conceptual connections. Graphic organizers, also known as word webs or semantic, mind, and concept maps, can be used to plan lessons or present information to students. Once familiar with the technique, students should be able to construct their own graphic organizers, reflecting their understanding of the concepts taught.

Because we live in a highly visual world, using visuals as a teaching strategy makes sense. Each day, students are overwhelmed with images from video games, computers, and television. Visual strategies capitalize specifically on the one modality that many students use consistently and have developed extensively—the visual modality. Types of visuals include overheads, maps, graphs, charts, and other concrete objects and artifacts that clarify learning. Because so much sensory input comes from visual sources, pictures, words, and learning-related artifacts around the classroom take on exaggerated importance in students' brains. Visuals such as these provide learning support and constant reinforcement.

These memorable strategies help students make sense of learning by focusing on the ways the brain learns best. Fully supported by the latest brain research, these strategies provide the tools you need to boost motivation, energy, and most important, the academic achievement of your students.

CHAPTER 1

Mathematics

Bear Paws: T-Chart

Skills Objectives

Demonstrate the meaning of addition.

Use addition to solve problems.

A **T-Chart** is a graphic organizer that can help students compare two items. Presenting a problem visually with the help of organizers and manipulatives makes it easier for students to perceive patterns. In this activity, students use a T-chart to visualize and solve an arithmetic problem.

Materials

Bear Paws reproducible

bear manipulatives

chart paper

1. Show students a bear manipulative. Ask them to find and count the bear's paws. Then show them another bear. Ask them to count the paws on both bears.

2. Tell students that they can use a T-chart to help them figure out how many paws the bears have. Draw a T-chart on chart paper and ask students to explain how this chart got its name. (It looks like the letter *T*.) Label the columns *How Many Bears?* and *How Many Paws?*

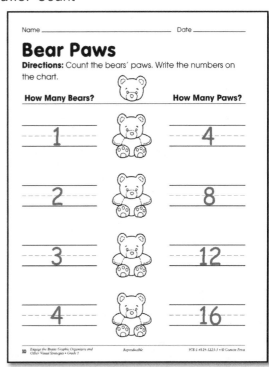

3. Show students one bear. Ask: *How many bears?* Have a volunteer write the number *1* on the chart. Then ask: *How many paws?* Count the paws as a class and have a volunteer write the number *4* on the chart.

4. Give each student a copy of the **Bear Paws reproducible (page 10)** and four bear manipulatives. Have students count the paws on the bear counters and record the results on the T-chart.

5. Once students have completed their charts, review the results. Have them look for a pattern. Help them see that the number of paws grows by four each time, and that two bears have twice as many paws as one bear.

Extended Learning

- Have students use the graphic organizer to chart the number of eyes or ears.
- Put copies of the reproducible in the math center. Have students use it to count beyond 16.

Name _____ Date _____

Bear Paws

Directions: Count the bears' paws. Write the numbers on the chart.

How Many Bears?		How Many Paws?
1		4
2		8
3		12
4		16

10 *Engage the Brain: Graphic Organizers and Other Visual Strategies • Grade 1*   *Reproducible*   978-1-4129-5223-5 • © Corwin Press

Name _____   Date _____

Bear Paws

Directions: Count the bears' paws. Write the numbers on the chart.

How Many Bears?		How Many Paws?
	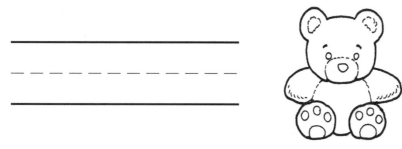	

Engage the Brain: Graphic Organizers and
Other Visual Strategies • Grade 1   Reproducible   978-1-4129-5225-5 • © Corwin Press

Who Has the Button? Venn Diagram

Skills Objectives

Sort items according to one attribute and multiple attributes.
Use a Venn diagram.

Materials
Button Sort
reproducible

yarn

buttons

index cards

scissors

Sorting items according to their characteristics is an essential math skill. A **Venn Diagram** is a graphic organizer that helps students discover how two items are different as well as what they have in common. Venn diagrams can be used to sort almost anything. In this activity, students use a Venn diagram to sort buttons.

1. Arrange two loops of yarn on the floor next to each other. Set out two different colors of buttons (e.g., white and black). Include some buttons with two holes and some with four holes.

2. Ask students: *How could we sort these buttons into two groups?* Lead them to see that one way they can sort is according to color. Label one circle *White* and the other one *Black*. Have volunteers help you sort the buttons according to these attributes.

3. Ask students: *How else could we sort the buttons?* Suggest sorting by the number of holes. Make labels reading *Two Holes* and *Four Holes*. With students' help, sort the same buttons according to these attributes.

4. Next, suggest that students sort the buttons into two more groups—buttons that are white and buttons that have two holes. Label the circles *White* and *Two Holes*. Begin sorting the buttons.

5. Students will soon realize that some buttons fit into both categories. Discuss possible solutions. Help students see that if they overlap the yarn loops, they can sort some buttons into both categories. Explain that the two overlapping circles is called a Venn diagram.

6. Give students a copy of the **Button Sort reproducible (page 12)**. Have them cut out the button shapes and then sort the buttons. Encourage students to sort the buttons as many ways as they can.

7. Have students take home their button sorting materials and share this activity with their families.

Button Sort

Directions: Cut out and sort the buttons. Tell how you sorted them.

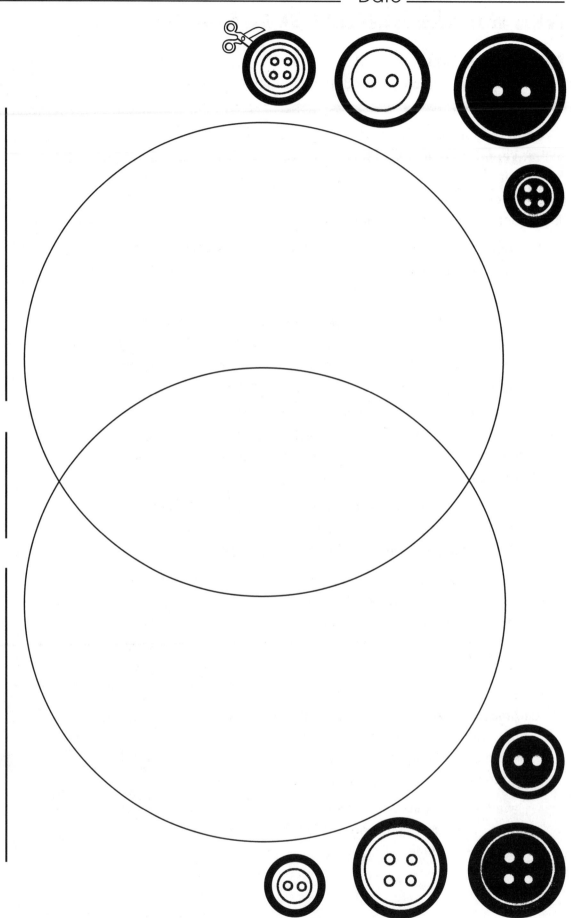

Tally Up! Tally Chart

Skills Objectives
Represent and understand numerical patterns.
Use tally marks to count objects.

Materials
Tally Up!
reproducible

Knowing how to organize and represent data is essential for success in science, math, social studies, and many other subject areas. A **Tally Chart** is an easy-to-use tool that has the extra benefit of exposing students to groupings of five. Once students know how to tally numbers, they will find many uses for this strategy.

1. Ask students: *How can we find out how many boys and how many girls are in the class?* List students' suggestions on the board.

2. Then ask: *How can we sort the boys and girls to make them easier to count?* Select a method as a class. Students might choose to have girls stand and boys sit, or to arrange themselves in two groups for easier counting.

3. Count aloud the girls in the class, and make a tally mark on the board to represent each girl. Tally the marks in groups of five, using a diagonal mark to mark the fifth entry in each group. Repeat to count the boys.

4. Count the tally marks with students, and then ask a volunteer to count the marks. Explain that they can count tally marks quickly by counting by fives. Check for understanding by having students count their classmates by fives.

5. Make many copies of the **Tally Up! reproducible (page 14)** and place them in the math center. Have students use the pages to tally the number of crayons, markers, and pencils in class or in their desks.

6. Invite students to discuss what they learned. Ask questions such as: *Do we have more pencils or crayons in the classroom? Which number is smallest? How did tally marks help you count?*

Extended Learning
Have students suggest other items to count and tally. Encourage them to chart their tally marks and compare the numbers.

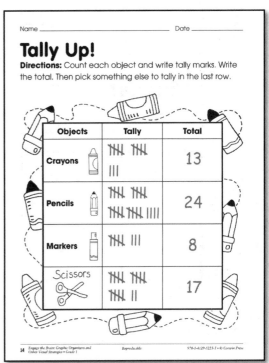

Name _____ Date _____

Tally Up!
Directions: Count each object and write tally marks. Write the total. Then pick something else to tally in the last row.

Objects	Tally	Total
Crayons	卌 卌 |||	13
Pencils	卌 卌 卌 卌 ||||	24
Markers	卌 |||	8
Scissors	卌 卌 卌 ||	17

14 *Engage the Brain: Graphic Organizers and Other Visual Strategies • Grade 1*   *Reproducible*   978-1-4129-5225-5 • © Corwin Press

Name _____   Date _____

Tally Up!

Directions: Count each object and write tally marks. Write the total. Then pick something else to tally in the last row.

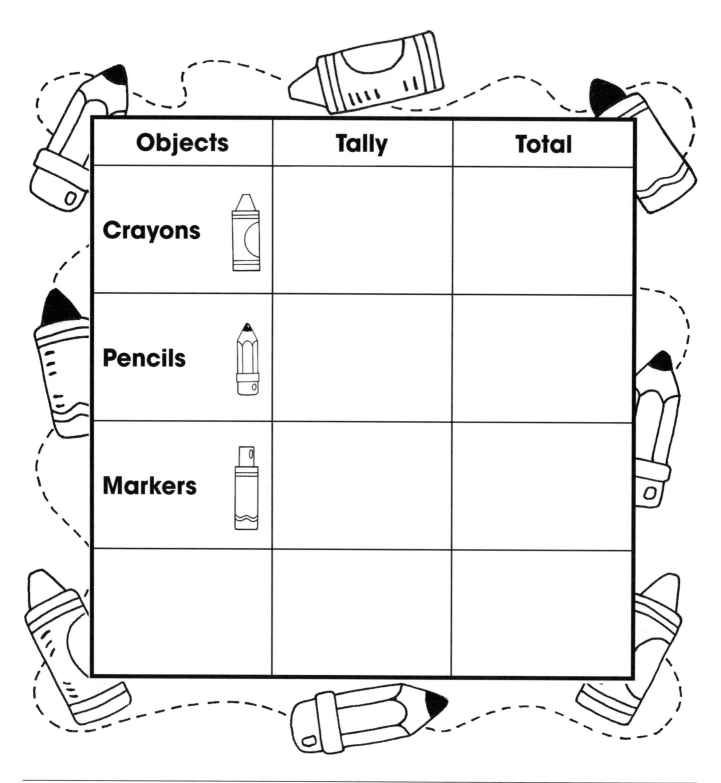

Objects	Tally	Total
Crayons		
Pencils		
Markers		

 Engage the Brain: Graphic Organizers and Other Visual Strategies • Grade 1   Reproducible   978-1-4129-5225-5 • © Corwin Press

Favorite Apples: Picture Graph

Skills Objective
Use concrete graphs and picture graphs as tools for representing information.

As students learn to visually represent data, they can begin to create graphs. In a **Concrete Graph**, objects are used to show data. In a **Picture Graph**, pictures represent the data. In this activity, students create both kinds of graphs.

1. Draw a 3 x 20 grid on a strip of butcher paper. Make boxes about four inches square. Label the three rows *Red, Green,* and *Yellow.*

2. Place the grid on the floor and invite students to gather around it. Ask them to sort the apples according to color, and place the apples on the grid. Ask questions about the graph to guide students' thinking: *Which group has the most apples? Which has the least?*

3. Wash the apples and slice them into wedges, leaving on the peels. Give one wedge of each color apple to each student.

4. Have students taste the three apples and choose a favorite. Then give them a copy of the **My Favorite Apple reproducible (page 16)**. Have students color the apple shape on the page to indicate their favorite type of apple and then cut it out.

5. Gather around the floor grid again. This time, have students graph their favorite apple using their colored apple shapes.

6. Discuss the results with students. *Which apple was the favorite? How many students chose red apples as their favorite? Which apple is the least favorite?*

Extended Learning
- Have students use the grid to graph other favorites, such as ice cream flavors, colors, or pets. Write new labels on sentence strips and place them on the grid. Students can draw their favorites and add them to the grid to make a picture graph.

- Ask students to write one or two words to describe their favorite apple.

Name _____ Date _____

My Favorite Apple
Directions: Write your name on the apple. Color it to match the color of your favorite apple. Cut out the apple and place it on the class graph.

Emily

16 *Engage the Brain: Graphic Organizers and Other Visual Strategies • Grade 3*   *Reproducible*   978-1-4129-5225-5 • © Corwin Press

My Favorite Apple

Directions: Write your name on the apple. Color it to match the color of your favorite apple. Cut out the apple and place it on the class graph.

978-1-4129-5225-5 • © Corwin Press

Things We Like: Bar Graph

Skills Objectives
Conduct a survey.
Represent data graphically.

Materials
Things We Like reproducible

overhead projector

transparency

A **Bar Graph** is used to compare items that can be counted. The horizontal scale along the bottom shows what is being counted. The vertical scale shows the number of items in each category. A bar graph makes it easier for students to see and compare data.

1. Lead students in a discussion about the sports they enjoy playing or watching. As students brainstorm sports, list their ideas on the board.

2. Review the list with students. Then ask each student to identify a favorite sport from the list. Ask: *How can we figure out which sport is our class favorite?* Students might suggest lining up according to favorite sport, taking a show of hands, or making a tally chart. Count the students in each category, and record the results.

3. Display an overhead transparency of the **Things We Like reproducible (page 18)**. Demonstrate how to enter the name of each sport on the horizontal scale. Then model how to graph the data by filling in the squares.

4. Check understanding by asking questions such as: *Which bar is tallest? What does that tell you? Which bar is shortest? Did more students like soccer or basketball?*

5. Ask students another survey question, such as: *What is your favorite book?* or *What is your favorite zoo animal?* Tally the results on the board.

6. Write the categories in the horizontal scale of the reproducible, and then make a photocopy for each student. Instruct students to graph the survey results.

7. When students are finished, talk about the different kinds of graphs that students have used or seen. Discuss pie charts, line graphs, pictographs, and so on.

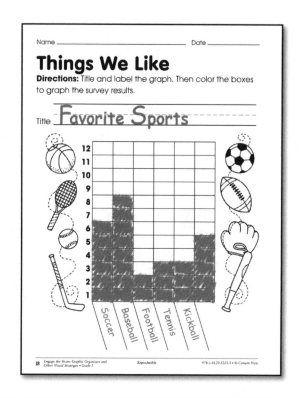

Things We Like

Directions: Title and label the graph. Then color the boxes to graph the survey results.

_____

- -

Title _____

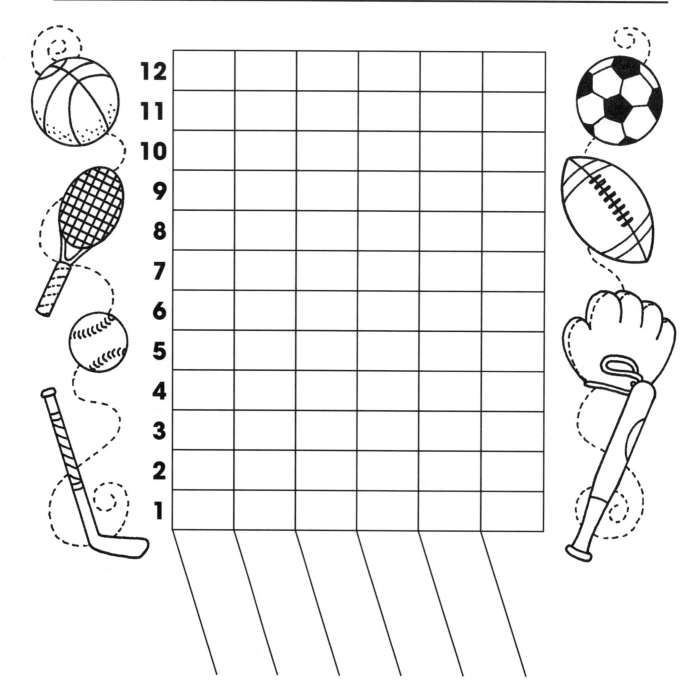

Add It Up: Number Line

Skills Objectives
Use a number line to add numbers.
Recognize number order.

Materials
Jump To It!
reproducible

masking tape

paper

pennies

dice

red and blue crayons

A **Number Line** provides students with a concrete reference for number sequence. Number lines can be used for number recognition, counting, addition, and subtraction. In this activity, students use a number line to add sums. They also learn that the order in which numbers are added has no effect on the solution.

1. Tape numbers from 0 to 12 on the floor, using one sheet of paper for each number to make a number line. Count the numbers as a class. Ask a volunteer to jump forward four spaces and then three more. Think aloud as the student jumps: *If you jump four spaces and then jump three spaces more, you land on seven.*

2. Ask another volunteer to jump three spaces and then four more. Help students realize that the results are the same (4 + 3 = 7 and 3 + 4 = 7). Continue with more examples. Encourage students to count aloud as they jump.

3. Give each student a copy of the **Jump To It! reproducible (page 20)**, a penny, and a pair of dice. Read the directions with students. Demonstrate how to roll one die, read the number (e.g., *2*), and move the penny that number of spaces. Then roll the other die, read the number (e.g., *6*), and move the penny again. Read the final number aloud (e.g., *8*).

4. Repeat the exercise, this time counting the numbers in the opposite order (e.g., *6* and *2*). Check understanding: *If I'm on number 6, and I jump two spaces more, what number will I land on?*

5. Have students continue rolling the dice and using the number line to find the sum. Have them take turns counting to discover that the order in which numbers are added has no effect on the sum.

6. As students work, ask questions to guide their thinking: *Which number will you count first? What would happen if you counted the other number first? How could you write it down? How would you teach a kindergartner to use a number line?*

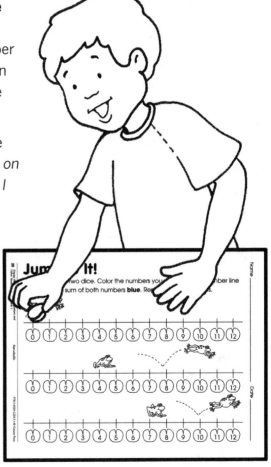

Name _____ Date _____

Jump To It!

Directions: Roll two dice. Color the numbers you roll on the first number line **red**. Color the sum of both numbers **blue**. Repeat two more times.

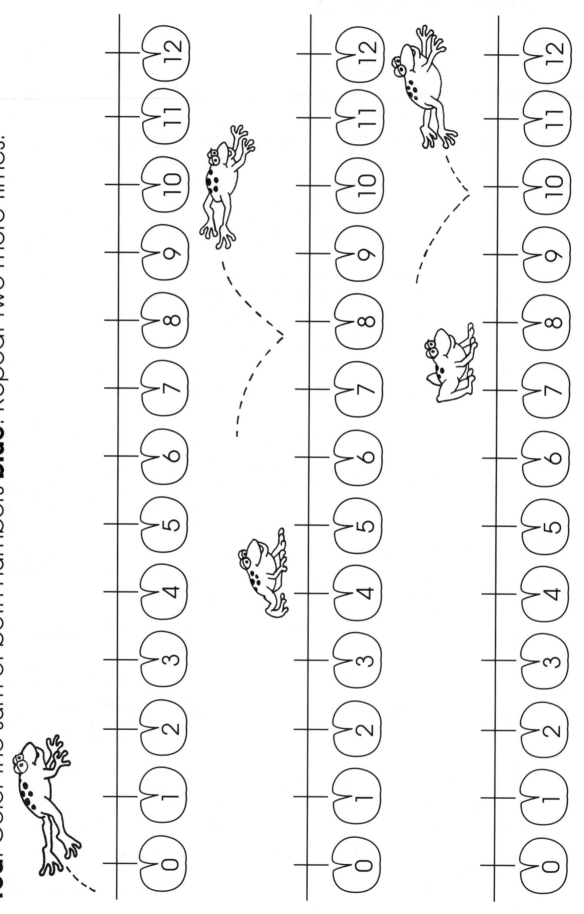

Engage the Brain: Graphic Organizers and Other Visual Strategies • Grade 1

Reproducible

How Long? Measurement Manipulatives

Skills Objective
Measure the length of objects using nonstandard units of measurement.

Making linear measurements is a skill students develop over time. Before using standard units of measurement, students should compare the lengths of objects and then measure with nonstandard units. **Measurement Manipulatives** can be used as nonstandard units to compare measurements of various objects. In this activity, students use paper clips and toothpicks to measure items in the classroom.

Materials
How Long Is It?
reproducible

pencil

paper clips

toothpicks

1. Review the meaning of the words *shorter* and *longer* with students. Show students a pencil. Have volunteers find items that are both longer and shorter than the pencil.

2. Point out that comparing two items tells us something about their size but doesn't give us all the information we need. For instance, both a paper clip and a crayon are shorter than a pencil, but knowing this doesn't tell the length of these items. Explain that measuring helps us find the length or width of items.

3. Tell students that they can use almost any objects of the same size to measure another object. Demonstrate how to use paper clips to measure the length of the pencil. Line up the paper clips end-to-end, count them, and write the number on the board. Then repeat the process using toothpicks.

4. Check for understanding by asking students: *Why did we use the paper clips to measure the pencil? How did we do it?*

5. Give each student paper clips, toothpicks, and a copy of the **How Long Is It? reproducible (page 22)**. Have students use the paper clips and toothpicks to measure items around the classroom and then record their results.

6. Have students meet in small groups to discuss results. Talk about why it takes more paper clips than toothpicks to measure an object and why the measurement of some objects (such as shoes) varies.

Extended Learning
Give some students small paper clips and others large paper clips. Ask them to explain why their measurements varied.

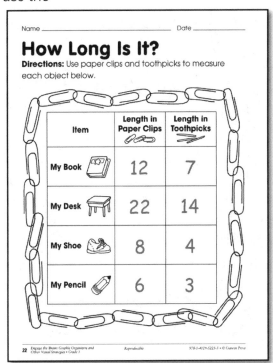

Name _____ Date _____

How Long Is It?
Directions: Use paper clips and toothpicks to measure each object below.

Item	Length in Paper Clips	Length in Toothpicks
My Book	12	7
My Desk	22	14
My Shoe	8	4
My Pencil	6	3

How Long Is It?

Directions: Use paper clips and toothpicks to measure each object below.

Item	Length in Paper Clips	Length in Toothpicks
My Book		
My Desk		
My Shoe		
My Pencil		

Picture the Problem: Picture Chart

Skills Objectives
Represent problems graphically.
Perform mathematical operations (addition, subtraction).

To solve a mathematical problem accurately, students must have a clear understanding of what the problem is asking them to do. Drawing a picture on a **Picture Chart** can be an effective strategy for clarifying a problem and visually representing its solution. Often, students can solve mathematical problems by drawing pictures before they can solve them as numerical equations.

Materials
Picture the Problem reproducible

Story Problems reproducible

index cards

glue

scissors

1. Write the following word problem on the board and read it aloud: *Casey had a pet cat. One day, his cat had 3 kittens. How many cats does Casey have now?*

2. Ask students to suggest how you might solve this problem. Lead them to conclude that you could draw a picture.

3. Read the problem again, and establish that the question is: *How many cats does Casey have now?* Draw a picture of a mother cat and three kittens on the board. Ask a volunteer to use the picture to explain the problem and solution. With students' help, write the problem as an equation: *1 + 3 = 4.*

4. Give students a copy of the **Picture the Problem reproducible (page 24)**. Write the following problem on the board: *Jan stacked 3 boxes. Dan stacked 4 boxes. How many boxes did they stack all together?*

5. Have students state the question and then use the reproducible page to draw a picture that represents the problem. Circulate as students work and help them write the problem as an equation.

6. Photocopy and glue story problems from the **Story Problems reproducible (page 25)** onto index cards. Place the cards and a stack of Picture the Problem reproducibles in the math center. Have students select a card and solve the problem by drawing a picture. They can trade papers with a partner to check their work.

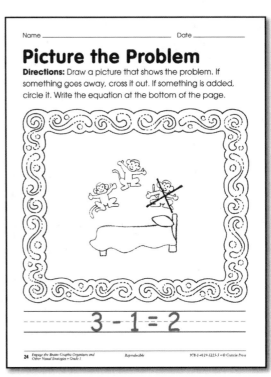

Name _____ Date _____

Picture the Problem
Directions: Draw a picture that shows the problem. If something goes away, cross it out. If something is added, circle it. Write the equation at the bottom of the page.

$$3 - 1 = 2$$

24 *Engage the Brain: Graphic Organizers and Other Visual Strategies • Grade 1*   Reproducible   978-1-4129-5225-5 • © Corwin Press

Picture the Problem

Directions: Draw a picture that shows the problem. If something goes away, cross it out. If something is added, circle it. Write the equation at the bottom of the page.

 Engage the Brain: Graphic Organizers and Other Visual Strategies • Grade 1   978-1-4129-5225-5 • © Corwin Press

Story Problems

3 monkeys are jumping on the bed. 1 fell off. How many monkeys are on the bed?

Cam and Cal swim. Sam and Sal ride bikes. How many children are there in all?

We need 11 kids for a soccer team. We have 9. How many more kids do we need?

Max picked 4 green apples and 2 red apples. He gave Kim 2 green apples. How many apples does Max have left?

Jan has 5 dogs. Ben has 3 dogs. How many dogs are there in all?

Min has 3 scoops. Tran has 3 scoops. How many scoops are there in all?

7 lions are roaring. 4 fell asleep. How many lions are roaring?

Frog has 6 flies. He ate 2. How many flies are left?

Math Vocabulary: Word Wall

Skills Objective

Use appropriate mathematical vocabulary.

A **Word Wall** is an interactive word bank. Word walls are often used for language arts activities, but they can be just as effective in other subject areas. A math word wall provides students with the vocabulary they need to write and talk about their mathematical thinking and serves as a visual reminder of important math symbols.

1. Select a bulletin board. Choose a means of organizing the words on the wall. You might choose to organize the words alphabetically, by category (numbers, addition and subtraction, measurement), or a combination of both.

2. Introduce the word wall by printing five words on sentence strips. Read the words to students, and then have students read them as a class. Talk about the meaning of each word, and ask volunteers to use each word in a sentence. Then place the words on the word wall.

3. Review the words on the word wall often and challenge students to use the words as they explain how they solve mathematical problems.

4. Add new words to the word wall frequently. As students learn new mathematical concepts, encourage them to suggest words to add to the wall.

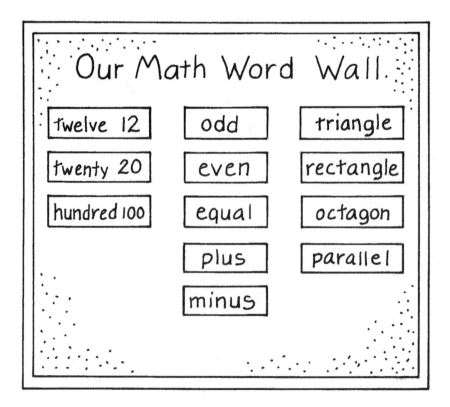

Our Math Word Wall.

twelve 12	odd	triangle
twenty 20	even	rectangle
hundred 100	equal	octagon
	plus	parallel
	minus	

CHAPTER 2

Science

Plants We Eat: Chart Matrix

Skills Objectives
Identify plant parts.
Name the function of plant parts.
Follow a written procedure.

A **Chart Matrix** is one of the most commonly used graphic organizers. Matrices are used to categorize and organize information. In this activity, students use a chart matrix to present information about plant parts.

1. Review with students the parts of a plant: stem, leaves, roots, flower, fruit, and seeds. Display a small plant or an illustration, and have students identify the parts. Discuss the function of each part.

2. Remind students that many of the foods we eat are parts of plants (i.e., fruits and vegetables). Display each fruit or vegetable, and discuss the part that we eat. Have students sort the produce according to the part that is eaten: leaves (lettuce); roots (carrots); flower (broccoli); seed (corn); fruit (apple).

Materials
Plants We Eat reproducible

small plant or illustration

lettuce, broccoli, carrot, corn, apple

chart paper

research materials (dictionaries, nonfiction books about plants)

crayons or markers

3. Ask students: *If we wanted to share this information with other people, how could we do it?* Guide students to understand that a chart is an effective way of presenting this information.

4. Draw a grid on chart paper. Print the following column headings: *Leaves, Roots, Flowers, Seeds, Fruit.* Print the names of the fruits and vegetables down the left column.

5. Ask volunteers to come to the chart and mark the appropriate column to show which part of each plant is eaten. Tell students that they will complete their own charts about plant parts we eat.

6. Give students a copy of the **Plants We Eat reproducible (page 29)**. Have them work in pairs to record five different fruits or vegetables down the left column. Encourage students to choose foods that will fit into various categories. Have them determine which part(s) of the plant is eaten, using sources such as dictionaries or nonfiction books about plants. Then invite students to complete their charts.

7. Have students share the results of their investigation with the class. Invite them to share which fruits and vegetables they enjoy the most and which ones they don't like.

Extended Learning

- With students, compile the information from all the charts into a larger class chart that shows all the plants and plant parts we eat. Help them sort the plant names in alphabetical order and then fill in the part of the plant that is eaten. Students may wish to use a computer for this activity.

- Bring in several fruits and vegetables from the class chart for students to sample. Many children may not have tried or even seen some of them! Invite the class to vote for their favorites.

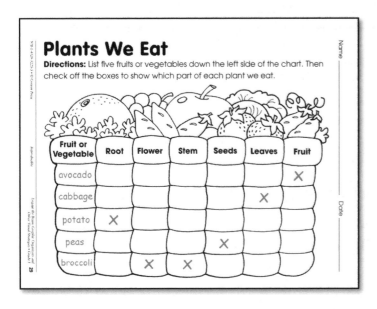

Plants We Eat

Directions: List five fruits or vegetables down the left side of the chart. Then check off the boxes to show which part of each plant we eat.

Fruit or Vegetable	Root	Flower	Stem	Seeds	Leaves	Fruit
avocado						X
cabbage					X	
potato	X					
peas				X		
broccoli		X	X			

Name _____ Date _____

Plants We Eat

Directions: List five fruits or vegetables down the left side of the chart. Then check off the boxes to show which part of each plant we eat.

Fruit or Vegetable	Root	Flower	Stem	Seeds	Leaves	Fruit

Salad Days: Recipe Chart

Materials

Salad Recipe Chart reproducible

fresh spinach

carrots (grated)

black beans (rinsed and drained)

green onions

golden raisins or dried currants

paper towels

plastic knives

salad bowls

salad dressing

Skills Objectives

Follow procedural steps.

Identify and describe plant parts.

Cooking is an engaging way to foster scientific skills in young children. By using a **Recipe Chart**, students follow procedural steps and observe changes. In this activity, students follow step-by-step directions to make a salad and learn about the parts of plants as they work.

1. Lead students in a discussion about the parts of plants that we eat. Display food from the materials list for students to examine. Ask students to help identify each edible plant part (spinach, leaves; carrots, roots; black beans, seeds; green onions, stems; raisins or currants, fruit from dried grapes).

2. Divide the class into small groups, and give each group the **Salad Recipe Chart (page 31)**. Read the chart together and discuss the steps. Provide each group with salad ingredients and kitchen equipment.

3. Invite students to follow the steps on the chart to prepare a salad.

Extended Learning

- Have students take home a copy of the recipe chart and prepare a salad for their family.

- Suggest that students create their own recipe chart for something they would like to eat.

Name _____ Date _____

Salad Recipe Chart

1. Wash your hands.

2. Wash the vegetables. Pat them dry with paper towels.

3. Tear the spinach into pieces. Put it in the salad bowl.

4. Cut the carrot and onion into little pieces. Put them in the salad bowl.

5. Add the beans.

6. Sprinkle on raisins or currants.

7. Pour salad dressing on top. Mix it up.

8. Enjoy your salad!

All About Animals: Cluster Map

Skills Objectives

Describe animal behavior using relevant details and key information. Identify the main idea and supporting details.

Materials

Main Idea Map reproducible

nonfiction books about animals

overhead projector

transparency

A **Cluster Map** shows a main idea (or topic) and supporting details (or related ideas). Cluster maps are useful tools to build students' comprehension of informational texts. Before using this map with students, make sure they understand the difference between a main idea and details.

1. In advance, copy the **Main Idea Map reproducible (page 33)** onto a transparency. Read aloud a nonfiction book about animals, such as *How Kittens Grow* by Millicent E. Selsam. Preview the book with students and focus their attention on main ideas and details.

2. After reading the book, ask: *What is this book mostly about?* Remind students that the topic a book is mostly about is the main idea. Display the Main Idea Map transparency on the overhead. Write the main idea (e.g., *Kittens are baby cats*) in the center of the map. Then ask: *What are some important facts that tell more about the main idea?* Write these details in the surrounding paw prints.

3. Give student pairs a copy of the Main Idea Map. Have pairs read a paragraph from a nonfiction book (a new text or one they have already read).

4. Have students write the main idea and details on their cluster map. Make sure they are applying strategies appropriately. Remind them to ask themselves: *What is this text mostly about? What important facts tell more about the main idea?*

5. Have students form small groups to compare their cluster maps. Talk about the main ideas and details that each pair identified.

Extended Learning

- Provide blank Main Idea Maps, and encourage students to use this graphic organizer when they read new texts.

- Have students use their completed Main Idea Maps to write a few sentences about the topic.

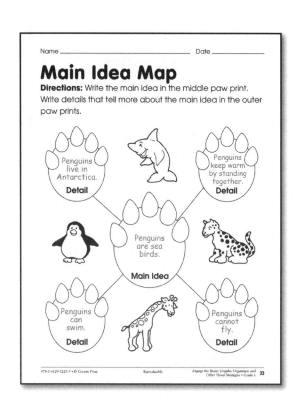

Name _____ Date _____

Main Idea Map

Directions: Write the main idea in the middle paw print. Write details that tell more about the main idea in the outer paw prints.

Penguins live in Antarctica. **Detail**

Penguins keep warm by standing together. **Detail**

Penguins are sea birds. **Main Idea**

Penguins can swim. **Detail**

Penguins cannot fly. **Detail**

978-1-4129-5225-5 • © Corwin Press   Reproducible   *Engage the Brain: Graphic Organizers and Other Visual Strategies • Grade 1* **33**

Main Idea Map

Directions: Write the main idea in the middle paw print. Write details that tell more about the main idea in the outer paw prints.

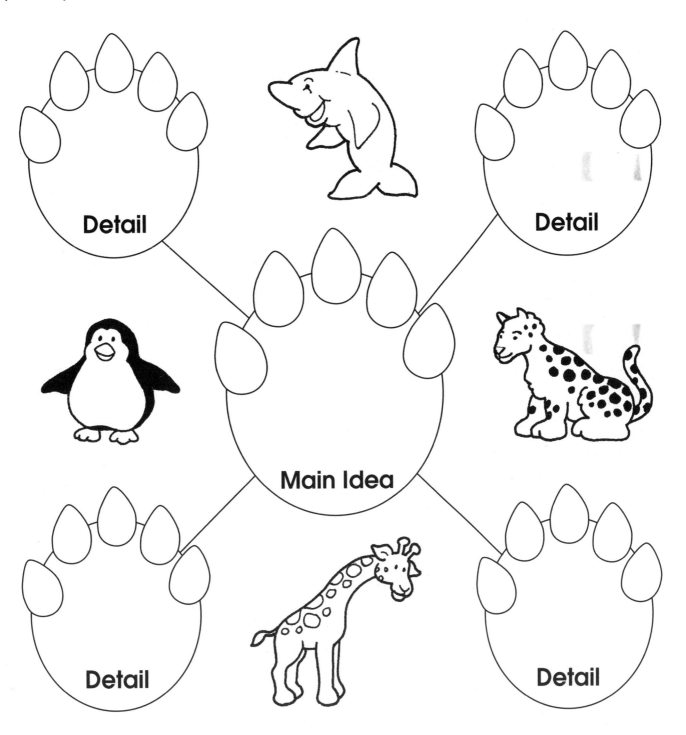

Animal Sort: Venn Diagram

Materials

Animal Picture Cards reproducible

Animal Characteristics Cards reproducible

scissors

hula-hoops

Skills Objectives

Classify animals according to physical and behavioral characteristics. Distinguish between similarities and differences.

Venn Diagrams are invaluable tools for classifying information. When students are first learning to classify, manipulatives such as picture cards can help make abstract concepts more concrete. In this activity, students use hula-hoops to classify animals according to physical and behavioral characteristics.

1. Photocopy the **Animal Picture Cards** and **Animal Characteristics Cards (pages 35–36)**, and cut out the cards. Show students the animal picture cards and review the name of each animal. Then show them the characteristics cards. Have volunteers read and define each word. Encourage them to mime the action words.

2. Place a hula-hoop on the floor. Select a characteristics card (e.g., *Has Fur or Hair*), read it aloud, and place it over the hoop. Have students find pictures of animals that share this characteristic (e.g., *zebra, kangaroo, seal, rabbit*), and place the cards in the hoop.

3. Set out another hula-hoop, and find a characteristics card that describes a behavior (e.g., *Swims*). Place the card over the hoop. Have students find pictures of animals that swim (e.g., *penguin, whale, turtle*), and place the cards in the hoop.

4. Ask students: *What about the seal? It has fur, and it swims. In which category does it belong?* Establish that the seal belongs in both categories. Demonstrate how to overlap the hoops to create a third section. Explain that the hoops form a Venn diagram, which shows how things are alike and how they are different.

5. Place another characteristics card over one of the hoops, and ask students if the animal cards still fit. Check for understanding.

6. Divide the class into small groups. Give each group two hoops, animal picture cards, and animal characteristics cards. Have students choose two characteristics cards, and sort the animal pictures into those groups.

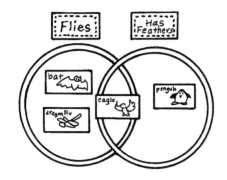

Extended Learning

- Set out the animal characteristics cards. Have students name or draw pictures of animals that fit in each category.

- Have students cut photos from nature magazines to make their own picture cards for this activity. Encourage them to write additional animal characteristics and classify them.

Animal Picture Cards

zebra

eagle

penguin

whale

kangaroo

seal

rabbit

bat

dragonfly

turtle

Animal Characteristics Cards

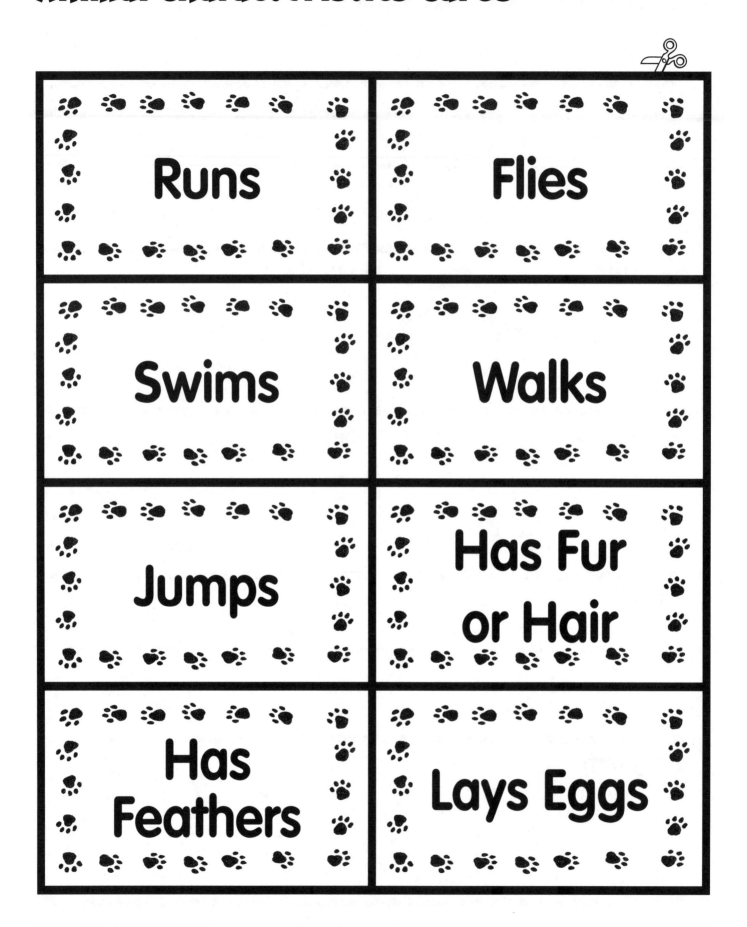

Runs

Flies

Swims

Walks

Jumps

Has Fur or Hair

Has Feathers

Lays Eggs

 Engage the Brain: Graphic Organizers and Other Visual Strategies • Grade 1   Reproducible   978-1-4129-5225-5 • © Corwin Press

Hiders and Trickers: T-Chart

Skills Objectives
Understand camouflage and mimicry.
Categorize animals using a chart.

Materials
nonfiction books
about animal
adaptations

Categorizing is an essential skill for young scientists. A **T-Chart** can help students categorize objects into two categories. In this activity, students learn about creatures that use camouflage or mimicry to avoid predators and then use a T-chart to classify them.

1. Read aloud a book about animal adaptations, such as *What Are Camouflage and Mimicry?* by Bobbie Kalman or *Why Do Tigers Have Stripes?* by Helen Edom.

2. Ask students to recall some of the animals from the book and list the ways that they protect themselves from danger. Establish that some animals, such as mule deer or katydids, have colorations that help them blend into their environments. Other animals, such as hawk moths that resemble snakes, trick predators by resembling other, more harmful creatures.

3. Draw a T-chart on the board with the headings *Hides* (camouflage) and *Tricks* (mimicry). Review the text with students, and help them categorize the animals according to their means of protection—camouflage or mimicry.

Hides	Tricks
bobcat	king snake
field mouse	owl butterfly
leaf insect	red salamander
walking stick	hawk moth

Extended Learning
- Have students draw pictures of how some of these animals use camouflage or mimicry to trick their predators (e.g., a tiger hiding in the tall grass, a leaf insect appearing like a leaf).

- Have students make T-charts to classify other animals, such as fish and mammals or reptiles and birds.

What's the Temperature? Table

Materials

What's the Temperature? reproducible

overhead projector

transparency

thermometers

masking tape

rulers

clipboards

Skills Objectives

Use a thermometer to record temperature.
Compare data.

A **Table** is a straightforward means of presenting data. Creating tables takes practice, as students must learn to locate data using column and row headings. In this activity, students record temperature data and then present it in a simple table.

1. Ask students how we know whether something is hot or cold. Establish that while there are many ways to determine this, one way is to use a thermometer.

2. Show students a thermometer, and demonstrate how to read the temperature. Ask: *Is the temperature the same on the playground as it is in our classroom? Is the ground the same temperature as the wall? Is the metal slide warmer or colder than the ground?* Discuss how students could find the answers to these questions, such as using a thermometer.

3. Copy the **What's the Temperature? reproducible (page 39)** onto a transparency, and display it on the overhead. Demonstrate how to read the column and row headings. Then fill in the indoor temperature for Day 1.

4. Help students tape a thermometer to a ruler and use the ruler as a stake to measure the temperature of the soil outside. Have them also tape a thermometer to the side of the school building and to a metal slide.

5. After about 30 minutes, help students read the temperature on the thermometers. Record the readings.

6. Write the thermometer readings on the board. Distribute copies of the What's the Temperature? reproducible, and have students copy their data onto the table.

7. Repeat the activity over the next two days, having students work independently to read and record the temperatures.

8. Interpret the table as a class. Ask students questions such as: *Was the temperature warmer in the classroom or outdoors? Which was colder—the ground or the slide?*

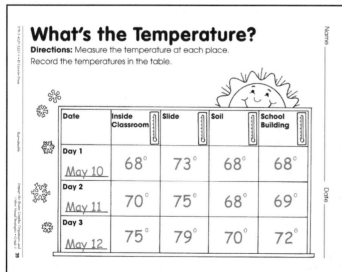

What's the Temperature?

Directions: Measure the temperature at each place. Record the temperatures in the table.

Date	Inside Classroom	Slide	Soil	School Building
Day 1 May 10	68°	73°	68°	68°
Day 2 May 11	70°	75°	68°	69°
Day 3 May 12	75°	79°	70°	72°

Name _____ Date _____

What's the Temperature?

Directions: Measure the temperature at each place.
Record the temperatures in the table.

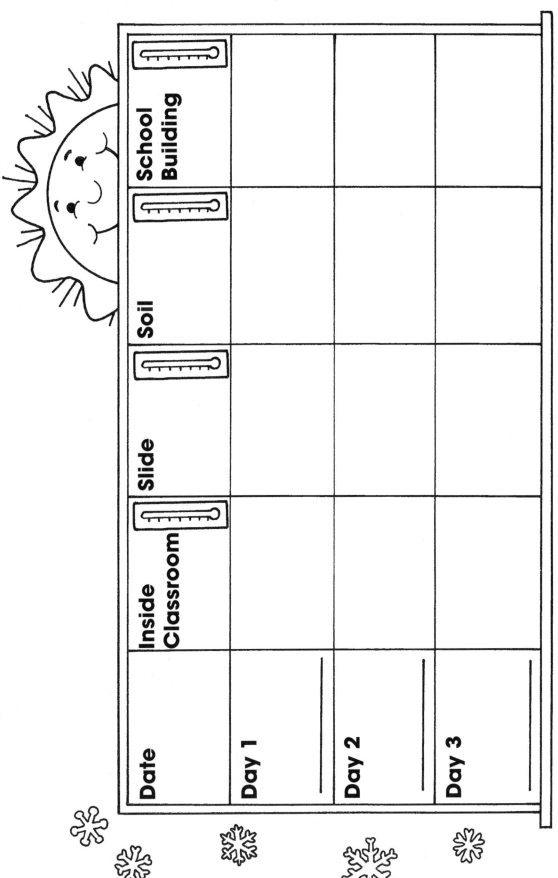

Date	Inside Classroom	Slide	Soil	School Building
Day 1				
Day 2				
Day 3				

Reproducible   *Engage the Brain: Graphic Organizers and*

Volcano! Chain of Events Map

Materials

Chain of Events Map reproducible

Volcano Experiment reproducible

overhead projector

transparency

carbonated water

food coloring

clear plastic cups

plastic trays

vinegar

baking soda

measuring cups

teaspoons

Skills Objectives

Conduct an experiment.
Observe and record events in sequence.

When students conduct experiments, a **Chain of Events Map** can help them see and record the steps in a process. Investigation is a linear process and requires procedural thinking. This tool can help students record the steps for any procedure.

1. Ask students: *What is an experiment?* List their ideas on the board. Discuss experiments that students have conducted or witnessed. Talk about why it is important for scientists to record the steps in an experiment. (So they can observe changes over time.)

2. Give students a copy of the **Chain of Events Map reproducible (page 42)**, and place a transparency of the reproducible on the overhead. Explain that this kind of map helps scientists to record the steps in an experiment.

3. Model how to use the map by conducting a simple demonstration for students. First, show students an empty cup and a bottle of carbonated water. Pour the water into the cup. Next, add a couple of drops of food coloring. Observe as the water changes color.

978-1-4129-5225-5

4. Record each step and the results on the transparency. At the conclusion of the experiment, have students retell the steps in their own words, using the Chain of Events Map as a guide.

5. Invite students to conduct their own experiment. Give each pair of students a copy of the **Volcano Experiment reproducible (page 43)**. Read the directions together. Have students follow the directions to make an erupting volcano. Then have them record the steps on their Chain of Events Map. (Note: Observe students carefully during this experiment. Solicit the help of parent volunteers or teacher aides to help, as needed.)

6. When students are finished, ask volunteers to share their maps with the class. Ask students: *How is this form useful?* (You can follow the directions in order and duplicate the steps of the experiment. Readers can learn about the results of an experiment without performing the experiment themselves.)

Extended Learning

Provide a stack of blank Chain of Events Maps in the science center. Invite students to write the steps of other experiments for their classmates to follow.

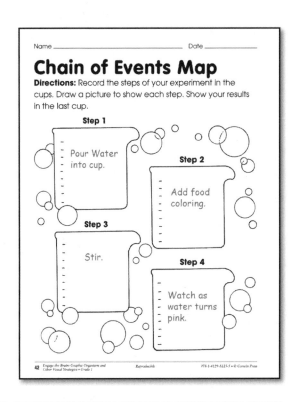

Chain of Events Map

Directions: Record the steps of your experiment in the cups. Draw a picture to show each step. Show your results in the last cup.

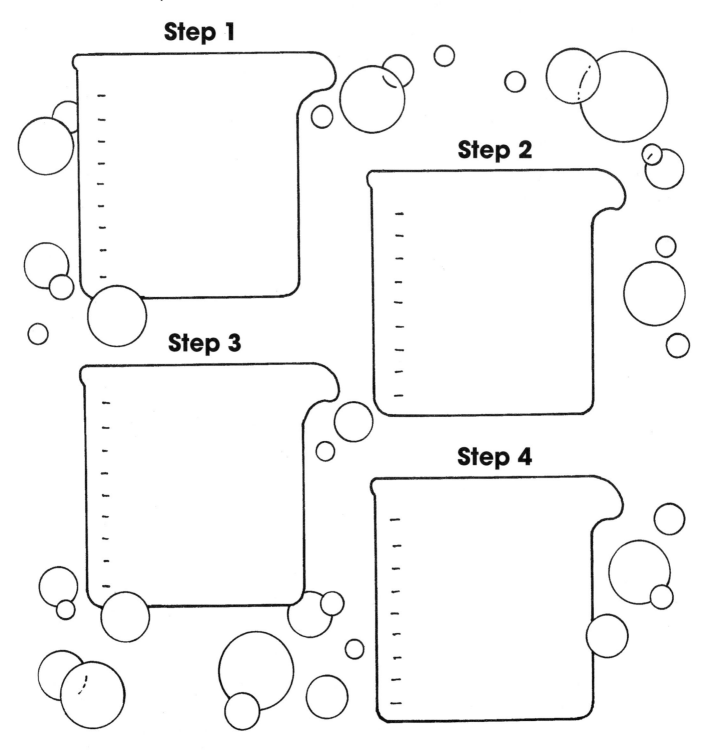

Step 1

Step 2

Step 3

Step 4

Name _____ Date _____

Volcano Experiment

Directions: Gather the materials. Read and follow the directions. Write and draw the steps on your Chain of Events Map.

You will need:
- clear plastic cup
- tray
- teaspoon
- measuring cup
- baking soda
- vinegar

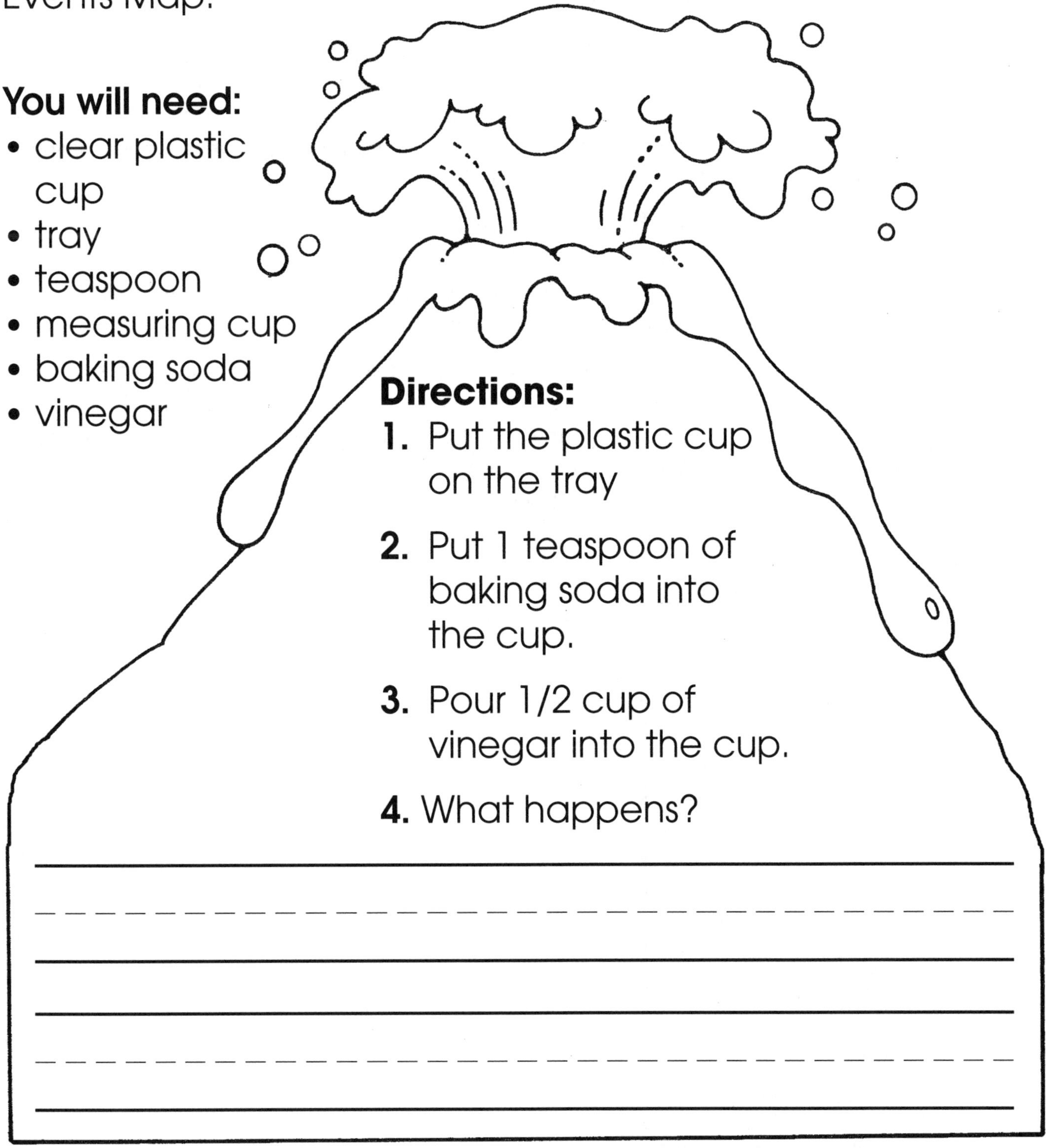

Directions:

1. Put the plastic cup on the tray

2. Put 1 teaspoon of baking soda into the cup.

3. Pour 1/2 cup of vinegar into the cup.

4. What happens?

_____

_____

_____

_____

Mind Pictures: Visualizing

Materials

My Mind Picture
reproducible

nonfiction books
about space travel

drawing paper

crayons or markers

Skills Objective

Use visualization as a strategy for comprehending science text.

As students learn to read content-area texts, **Visualizing** is an essential comprehension strategy. When students visualize, they combine what they already know (prior knowledge) with details from the text to create understanding.

1. Select a nonfiction book about space travel, such as *Me and My Place in Space* by Joan Sweeney to share with students. Turn to the first two pages. Read the words and point out the illustrations. Ask students to close their eyes and picture what happened when the space shuttle launched.

2. As students visualize, encourage them to relate details from the book to details from their own experience. Ask guiding questions, such as: *As you imagine the launch pad, how is it like other structures you have seen?*

3. Give students a copy of the **My Mind Picture reproducible (page 45)**. Distribute copies of the book, and have students reread it in small groups. Ask them to choose one sentence from the book and copy it at the top of the reproducible. Then have them draw what they visualized in the thought cloud.

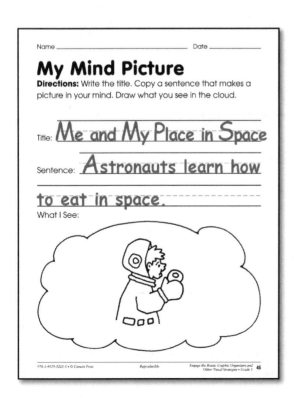

Name _____ Date _____

My Mind Picture

Directions: Write the title. Copy a sentence that makes a picture in your mind. Draw what you see in the cloud.

Title: _____

Sentence: _____

What I See:

CHAPTER 3

Social Studies

Factory Facts: Illustrations

Materials

illustrated nonfiction book about a factory

sticky notes

chart paper

Skills Objectives

Interpret illustrations.

Identify facts and make predictions.

As students read illustrated content-area text, they must think critically about what they are reading and learn to identify facts. Finding important details enables students to answer questions about the text and form conclusions and predictions. For young learners, facts and details may be found in both the text and the **Illustrations**.

1. Select an unfamiliar illustrated book about a factory, such as *What Happens at a Toy Factory?* by Kathleen Pohl to share with students. Cover the text with sticky notes and set the book aside. Ask students questions such as: *What comes to mind when you hear the word* factory? *What do you know about factories?*

2. Record students' ideas on a sheet of chart paper titled *What We Know About Factories.* For example: *They are big; They make things like crayons and cars; Lots of people work there; They make lots of the same thing.* Encourage students to expand on their ideas. Ask them to share details from prior experiences.

3. Show students the cover of the book. Ask for predictions about what the book will be about. Explain that you are going to look at the book but not read the words yet. Students will get information by looking at the illustrations.

4. Turn the pages of the book and pause to examine the illustrations. Ask students: *What do you think this picture is telling us about how toys are made? What makes you think so? Should we add this new information to our list of facts?*

5. After you finish previewing the illustrations, return to the list of facts about factories. Discuss what students already knew and what they learned from the illustrations. Ask students to suggest changes or deletions.

6. On a subsequent day, read aloud the text. As you review the text with students, revisit the list of facts. Together, add or delete information from the text.

All Kinds of Homes: Glyph

Skills Objectives
Compare and contrast different kinds of homes.
Interpret data on a glyph.

Materials
How to Make a Glyph reproducible

Glyph House reproducible

nonfiction books about houses

markers

A **Glyph** is a tool for representing data through pictures. Each element of a glyph represents a different fact. In this activity, students make a glyph that represents information about their home.

1. In advance, follow the directions on the **How to Make a Glyph reproducible (page 48)** to create your own glyph on the **Glyph House reproducible (page 49)**.

2. Share a nonfiction book about houses with students, such as *Houses and Homes* by Ann Morris. Encourage students to examine the illustrations as you read brief facts about how the type of shelter varies according to the region in which it is built.

3. Encourage students to think about the homes in their own community. Ask them what materials were used to build their houses and if there are other homes exactly like theirs. Talk about how homes reflect the people who live in them.

4. Tell students that they can share information about their home by making a glyph, a picture that gives information using symbols. Show students your completed glyph, and discuss what each item and color represents.

5. Distribute copies of the Glyph House reproducible. Read the directions aloud to students while they complete their own glyph.

6. When students are finished, have them meet in small groups to discuss and interpret their glyphs. Have groups discuss questions such as: *What materials were used to make the homes in our group? Which person has the biggest family? Does anyone share a bedroom?*

7. Choose one of the glyphs and show it to the class. Ask students to interpret the glyph and try to figure out who created it.

Extended Learning
Send a copy of both reproducibles home with each student. Parents can complete a glyph about their childhood home and compare it with their child's glyph.

Name _____ Date _____

Glyph House
Directions: Follow the directions to color the house.

How to Make a Glyph

1. If your home is made of wood, color the door **green**. If your home is made of brick or stone, color the door purple. If your home is made of a different material, color the door white.

2. If you have your own room, color the roof **brown**. If you share a room, color the roof **orange**.

3. If you walk to school, color the windows **green**. If you take a bus or a car to school, color the windows **orange**.

4. If you have a fireplace, color the chimney **red**. If you do not have a fireplace, color the chimney **green**.

5. If you live in a house, color the house **blue**. If you live in an apartment, color the house **red**. If your home is not a house or an apartment, color the house **yellow**.

6. Draw one tree for each member of your family.

 Engage the Brain: Graphic Organizers and Other Visual Strategies • Grade 1   *Reproducible*   978-1-4129-5225-5 • © Corwin Press

Glyph House

Directions: Follow the directions to color the house.

Jobs People Do: T-Chart

Materials

Goods and Services reproducible

purse

ruler

stapler

nonfiction book about jobs

crayons or markers

Skills Objective

Identify and categorize goods and services.

A **T-Chart** is a graphic organizer used to classify information into two categories. This simple chart can help students clarify understanding of a concept or compare and contrast two topics. In this activity, students use a T-chart to classify jobs that produce goods and those that produce services.

1. Hold up a purse, a ruler, and a stapler. Tell students that these are all goods. Ask if they know what a *good* is. Explain that a good is something people make or produce that they can sell. Brainstorm a list of goods with students, such as *toys, computers,* and *cars.*

2. Ask students if they can tell you what a *service* is. Explain that a service is something people do to help other people, such as teaching (teacher) or helping sick animals (veterinarian). Brainstorm a list of services.

3. Read aloud a nonfiction book about jobs, such as *Things People Do* by Ann Civardi and Stephen Cartwright. As you read the text and look at the pictures, ask students to notice whether each job provides goods or services.

4. Draw a T-chart on the board. Title the columns *Goods* and *Services*. Ask students to name some of the jobs from the book and decide whether each job provides goods or services. Sort the jobs according to these categories.

5. Ask students to think about the jobs people do in their families and neighborhoods. Give them a copy of the **Goods and Services reproducible (page 52)**. Invite them to draw pictures or write the names of jobs their family and neighbors do under the appropriate headings.

Extended Learning

- Suggest that students interview a family member about his or her job. As a class, compose a few interview questions such as: *What is the name of your job? What kinds of things do you do in your job? What do you like about your job?* Write out the interview questions and send them home with students. Have students determine whether the job provides a good or a service to others. Afterward, have them meet in small groups to discuss their interview subjects and their jobs.

- Have each student write the name and title of their interview subject on a sticky note. Draw a T-chart on chart paper, and have students place their sticky notes in the appropriate columns. Together, review the chart and talk about the goods and services people provide. Invite students to share which jobs they might want to pursue someday and why.

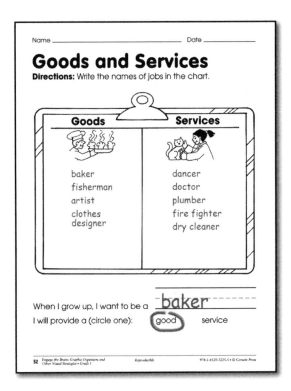

Goods and Services

Directions: Write the names of jobs in the chart.

Goods	Services

When I grow up, I want to be a _____

I will provide a (circle one):   good   service

Field Trip Fun: KWL Chart

Skills Objectives
Use prior knowledge.
Organize and categorize ideas.

Materials
chart paper

When approaching a new concept, using a graphic organizer can help students organize prior knowledge and a plan for learning. In this activity, students use a **KWL Chart** to prepare for and review a field trip.

1. A day or two before a field trip, draw a KWL chart on chart paper to work on as a class. Explain that the *K* stands for what students already *know* about a topic. The *W* stands for what they *want* to learn. The *L* stands for what they *learned*.

2. Remind students where they are going on their field trip. Explain that today you will fill out the first two columns of the KWL chart about the trip. Ask students to brainstorm everything they know about their field trip. Write their ideas in the *What We Know* column.

Field Trip: Baseball Stadium		
What We Know	**What We Want to Learn**	**What We Learned**
• a big building downtown • our team plays there • sells hot dogs • has bullpen • need tickets to get in • has a scoreboard	• Where do the players get ready? • Will we be able to go on the field? • Where do players sleep? • How much do tickets cost? • Can we get any autographs? • How old do you have to be to be a ball boy?	

3. Have students tell you what they want to learn during the field trip. Write questions in the *What We Want to Learn* column. Read the list of questions together, and copy them to bring on the trip.

4. After the field trip, review with students what they learned. Write answers to their questions and any other information learned in the *What We Learned* column.

Our School Museum: Visual Display

Materials

Artifact Cards reproducible

chart paper

disposable cameras (optional)

cardstock

scissors

glue

Skills Objectives

Plan and create a classroom museum.

Develop problem-solving and classification skills.

Creating a **Visual Display** challenges students to select, organize, and describe objects. In this activity, ideal for a unit on community, students choose and classify appropriate "artifacts" for a school museum.

1. Ask students about the kinds of museums they have visited. Explain that a museum is a place where people can learn by looking at artifacts, or things that people made a very long time ago. Behind the scenes at a museum, workers choose artifacts to display, and they explain why these items are important.

2. Tell students that they are going to plan a museum to help people learn about their school. Draw a simple idea web on chart paper. Title the web *Our School Museum*. Help students brainstorm different areas of the school, and record them in the big circles on the web (e.g., *playground, cafeteria, auditorium, library, classrooms*).

3. Then ask students to list items that might be found in each place. Record those ideas in the smaller circles connected to each larger circle on the web (e.g., *playground—swings, sports balls, four-square court, grass*).

4. Have students choose one area of the school and find an artifact to represent that area. Artifacts might include: a trophy or uniform for a sports team, a program from a school play or other performance, a menu from the school cafeteria, or a bookmark from the school library. If possible, provide disposable cameras, and have students take photographs of people and places around the school.

5. Photocopy enough of the **Artifact Cards reproducible (page 56)** so each student gets a card. Have students fill in the information about their artifact and glue the card to a piece of cardstock for durability.

6. Prompt students to arrange their artifacts and cards on their desks. Then invite the class to wander through the classroom to see all the school artifacts. (You may want to group together students who are displaying artifacts from the same area of the school.)

7. Invite other classes and parents to tour your School Museum. Students can conduct guided tours while telling about each artifact and its importance to the school.

Extended Learning

- Photograph the school museum, and compile the photos into a class book that includes students' artifact cards.

- To build background knowledge and understanding, have students explore Web sites for local and national museums.

- If possible, take your class on a field trip to a local community museum. Invite students to make mental notes of their favorite artifacts. Back in the classroom, ask students to share which artifacts they enjoyed the most and why.

Artifact Cards

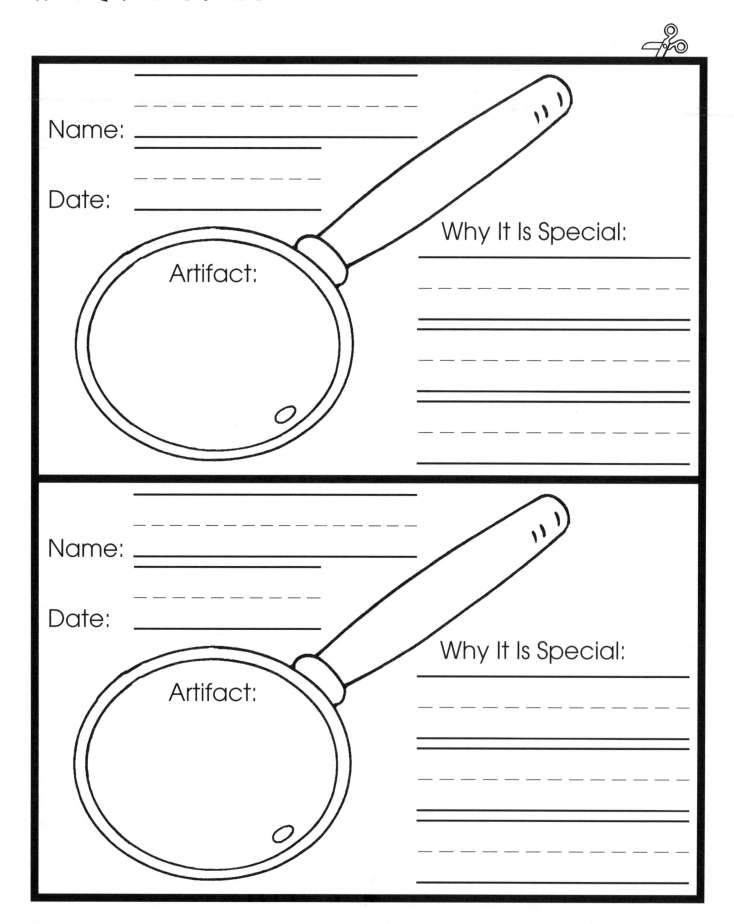

Name: _____

Date: _____

Artifact:

Why It Is Special:
_____
_____
_____
_____

Name: _____

Date: _____

Artifact:

Why It Is Special:
_____
_____
_____
_____

Rules and Consequences: Cause-and-Effect Chart

Skills Objectives

Describe the importance of rules.

Recognize the consequence, or effect, of certain actions.

Materials

Rules for Our School reproducible

One of the most critical concepts students can learn about rules is that when a rule is broken, there will be consequences. Using a **Cause-and-Effect Chart** helps make the relationship between broken rules and consequences more explicit for students.

1. Ask students why we have rules. Lead students to understand that rules are very important for our communities. They help keep people safe. We follow rules in school, at home, when we drive, and in many other situations.

2. Have a volunteer name a classroom rule. Write the rule on the board. Ask students why that rule is important and what happens when someone breaks that rule. Explain that a consequence is what happens when someone doesn't follow a rule.

3. Have students brainstorm a list of places in the school where they must follow rules. These might include the playground, the library, the cafeteria, the classroom, or the computer lab.

4. Divide the class into small groups. Assign each group a different area of the school, and give them a copy of the **Rules for Our School reproducible (page 58)**. Have group members list the rules for their area on the chart. Then have them discuss each rule and record the reason for the rule and the consequence for breaking it.

5. Have groups share their charts with the class. Together, compile a class chart of rules and consequences.

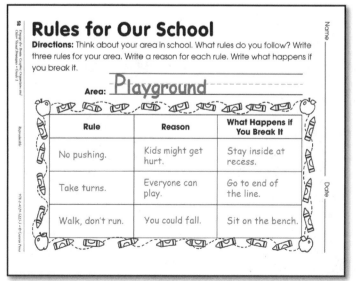

Rules for Our School

Directions: Think about your area in school. What rules do you follow? Write three rules for your area. Write a reason for each rule. Write what happens if you break it.

Area: Playground

Rule	Reason	What Happens if You Break It
No pushing.	Kids might get hurt.	Stay inside at recess.
Take turns.	Everyone can play.	Go to end of the line.
Walk, don't run.	You could fall.	Sit on the bench.

Name _____ Date _____

Rules for Our School

Directions: Think about your area in school. What rules do you follow? Write three rules for your area. Write a reason for each rule. Write what happens if you break it.

Area: _____

Rule	Reason	What Happens if You Break It

From Farm to Home: Flowchart

Skills Objectives
Describe how milk gets from the farm to home.
Identify and summarize steps in a process.

As students learn to read informational text, it is essential for them to understand steps in a process. A **Flowchart** graphic organizer can help students clarify what happens first, next, and last.

1. Ask students to think about where milk comes from and share their ideas. Tell them that they will read a book that explains more about the process.

2. Make copies of the **Milk Book reproducibles (pages 60–61)**. Make enough books so each student or group has their own. Fold the pages on the lines so page 1 is on top for the first page and page 3 is on top for the second page, as shown. Slide the second page into the first page to make an eight-page booklet. Staple the left side. Read the text and discuss the illustrations together.

3. After reading, ask students how the milk gets from the farm to their house. Assist them in retelling the steps in sequential order. Ask: *What happens first? What happens next?* List students' suggestions on the board in numerical order.

4. Explain that a flowchart is one way of showing the order of steps in a process. Give students a copy of the **Milk Flowchart reproducible (page 62)**. Explain that the arrows and numbers show the order of steps. Model how to fill in the first step of the flowchart. Then have students fill in the rest, using words and pictures.

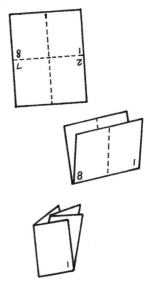

Extended Learning
- Read a milk carton with students. Help them find the definition of such words as *homogenized* and *pasteurized*.

- Make a class poster that shows all the products that can be made from milk.

- Have students use a flowchart to show how other items get produced, such as corn, apples, meat, eggs, or cotton clothing.

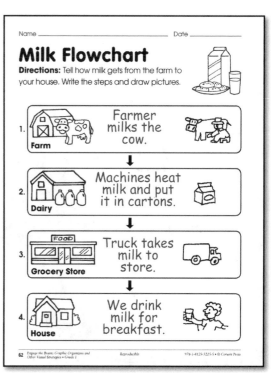

Milk Book

8 Milk tastes great!

This is Farmer Cam.
This is her cow, Sal. **1**

7 Dad takes us to the store
to buy milk.

Farmer Cam milks Sal with
a milking machine. **2**

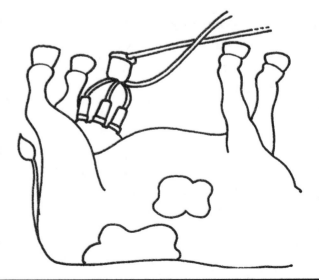

Milk Book

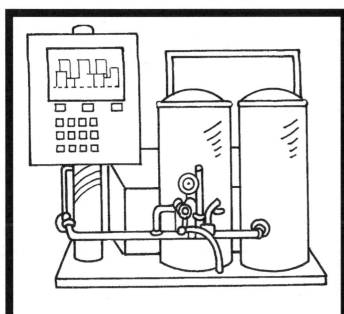

A machine heats the milk
4 to make it safe to drink.

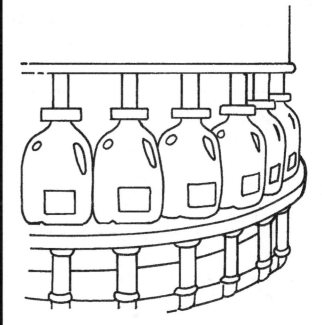

Then the milk is put
into bottles. **5**

3 A big truck takes the milk
to a dairy.

6 At last, the truck takes
the milk from the dairy to
the grocery store.

Milk Flowchart

Directions: Tell how milk gets from the farm to your house. Write the steps and draw pictures.

1.
Farm

2.
Dairy

3.
Grocery Store

4.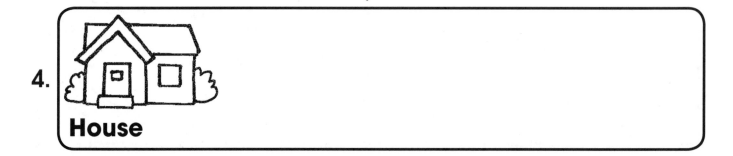
House

Mapping Our School: Maps

Skills Objectives
Read a map of the school grounds.
Identify fire safety features.
Make a map.

Materials
Fire Map
reproducible

school maps

Reading a **Map** is important for visual literacy. Understanding the relationship between three-dimensional space and a two-dimensional map takes practice. Expose students to all sorts of maps, and find ways to make maps relevant to students' lives. In this activity, students make and use maps to develop a plan for fire safety at their school.

1. Engage students in a discussion about fire safety. Ask them where they should exit the classroom during a fire drill. Point out that knowing the location of exits and fire alarms can help keep us safe.

2. Give students copies of a school map or building plan. Lead them on a walk around the school, and model how to mark the location of fire exits, fire extinguishers, and fire alarms on the map. Explain that map symbols show larger objects. Use *EXIT* for fire exits, a red triangle for fire extinguishers, and a red circle for fire alarms.

3. Ask students to imagine that they are birds flying above the school and looking down on it. Explain that this is called a "bird's-eye view." Point out the various features of the map and help students imagine how they look from above.

4. Back in the classroom, guide students in drawing a map of the classroom. Draw an outline of the classroom on the board. Focus on one area, such as the writing center, and model how to draw the area from above.

5. Give students a copy of the **Fire Map reproducible (page 64)**, and direct them to make a map of their classroom. Remind them to imagine that they are floating above the room and looking down.

6. Have students share their maps in groups. Ask: *How could we use these maps to keep ourselves safe?* Ask students to look around the classroom and locate the fire exit, fire alarms, and fire extinguishers. Have them add these features to their map.

Extended Learning
Have students and their families make fire escape maps for their own homes.

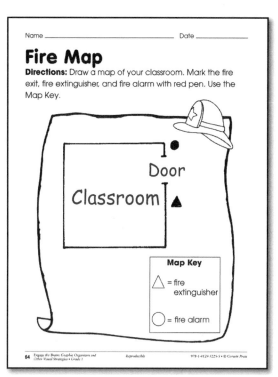

Name _____ Date _____

Fire Map
Directions: Draw a map of your classroom. Mark the fire exit, fire extinguisher, and fire alarm with red pen. Use the Map Key.

Door

Classroom

Map Key

△ = fire extinguisher

○ = fire alarm

64 *Engage the Brain: Graphic Organizers and Other Visual Strategies • Grade 1*   Reproducible   978-1-4129-5225-5 • © Corwin Press

Fire Map

Directions: Draw a map of your classroom. Mark the fire exit, fire extinguisher, and fire alarm with red pen. Use the Map Key.

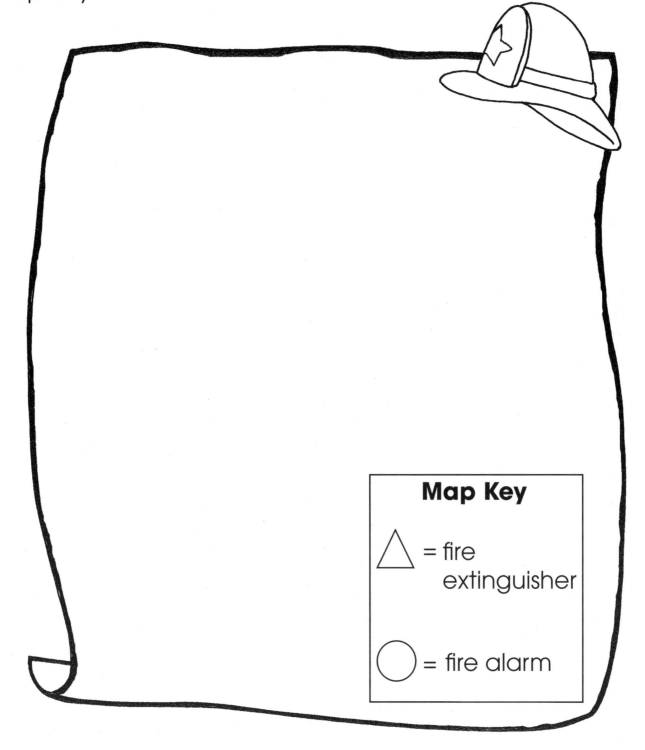

Map Key

△ = fire extinguisher

○ = fire alarm

CHAPTER 4

Language Arts

Meet This Book: Prediction Sheet

Skills Objective
Use picture and text clues to make predictions about text.

Effective readers use strategies, such as prediction, for approaching unfamiliar texts. Recording predictions on a **Prediction Sheet** can help students make connections to the text and set a purpose for reading.

1. Show students an unfamiliar book, such as *Wemberly Worried* by Kevin Henkes. Explain that previewing a book and making predictions are ways of figuring out what the story might be about.

2. Read the title of the book (e.g., *Wemberly Worried*) with students and look at the front cover illustration. Think aloud: *I wonder if the mouse on the cover is Wemberly? She looks worried.* Turn to the back cover and read the text. Discuss the back cover illustration.

3. Turn to the title page. Read the text and show the illustration. Ask students to share their thoughts.

4. Turn to the first page of the book. Read aloud the first few lines of text: *Wemberly worried about everything.* Think aloud about the text and illustration: *I wonder what sorts of things she worried about? I can see that this is the same bunny she is holding on the cover.*

5. Explain to students that by looking at the pictures, they can figure out more about the story. Preview the illustrations, encouraging students to share their observations.

6. Have students work with a partner as they preview an unfamiliar book. Have them record their observations on the **Meet This Book reproducible (page 66)**.

7. After students complete their pages, read the stories with them. Reflect on how previewing and predicting helped them understand the reading.

Materials
Meet This Book reproducible

unfamiliar picture books

Name _____ Date _____

Meet This Book
Directions: Look at your book. Write four clues you see. Then tell what you think will happen in the story.

Title: **Wemberly Worried**

Clue #1
Mouse looks worried.

Clue #2
She goes to a party.

Clue #3
She goes to school.

Clue #4
She worried about everything.

Name _____ Date _____

Meet This Book

Directions: Look at your book. Write four clues you see.
Then tell what you think will happen in the story.

_____
- -

Title: _____

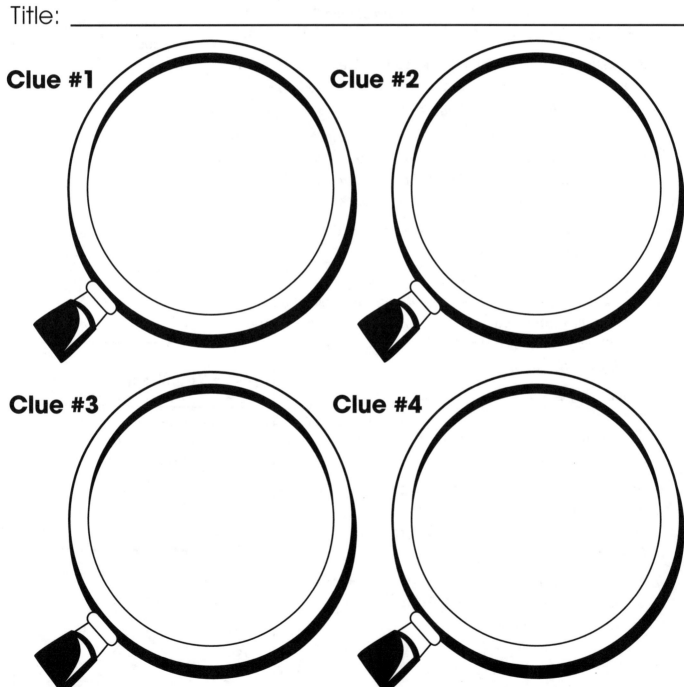

Clue #1

Clue #2

Clue #3

Clue #4

 *Engage the Brain: Graphic Organizers and
Other Visual Strategies* • Grade 1   Reproducible   978-1-4129-5225-5 • © Corwin Press

What's the Main Idea? Idea Web

Skills Objective
Identify the main idea and details in a story.

Materials
What's the Main Idea? reproducible

picture book

Knowing how to identify the main idea in a story is one of the more challenging comprehension tasks for young learners. It is also one of the most important. In order to master this skill, students need ample practice. An **Idea Web** can help students link a topic or main idea with supporting ideas or details.

1. Begin by showing students an illustration from a story. Ask: *What is this picture about?* List students' ideas on the board. Help students summarize their ideas, for example: *This picture is about two friends reading together.* Explain that this is a *main idea.*

2. Ask students: *What little bits of information also tell us about this picture?* Again, list students' ideas on the board. Explain that these little bits of information, called *details*, tell more about the main idea.

3. Tell students that as you read a story, they should think about the main idea. Write the title of the book on the board, and then read the book aloud.

4. When you're done reading, ask students: *What was this story mostly about?* Give them a copy of the **What's the Main Idea? reproducible (page 68)**. Draw a simple idea web on the board, and model how to record the main idea in the larger circle.

5. Then ask what bits of information, or details, tell more about the main idea. Write students' suggestions in the smaller circles. Check for understanding by giving an example from the story and asking if it's a detail or main idea.

6. Then read aloud another book to the class, such as *Pete's a Pizza* by William Steig. Invite students use their What's the Main Idea? reproducible to record the main idea and details. Remind them that they can use both words and pictures.

Extended Learning
Encourage students to use ideas from their idea webs to discuss the story. Ask questions such as: *Why do you think the author wrote this story? Why is it important to know what a story is mostly about?*

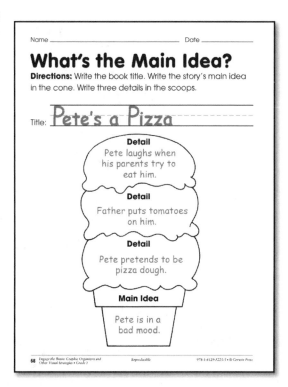

Name _____ Date _____

What's the Main Idea?

Directions: Write the book title. Write the story's main idea in the cone. Write three details in the scoops.

_____

Title: _____

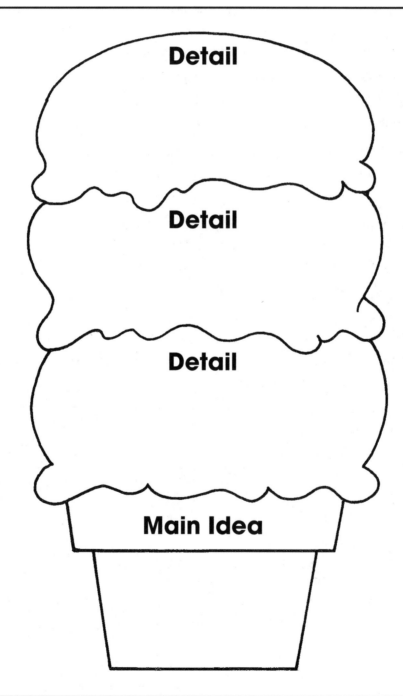

 Engage the Brain: Graphic Organizers and Other Visual Strategies • Grade 1   Reproducible   978-1-4129-5225-5 • © Corwin Press

Friends Like These: Character Comparison Chart

Skills Objectives
Identify and analyze character traits.
Compare two story characters.

Materials
Character Comparison Chart reproducible

Frog and Toad Are Friends by Arnold Lobel

overhead projector

transparency

Learning how to identify the similarities and differences between characters, setting, or plot enables students to better understand text and also prepares them to develop comparisons in their own writing. A **Character Comparison Chart** offers students a tool for making comparisons between characters, so they are easier to understand and visualize.

1. Ask students how they are like their friends and how they are different. Tell students that they will read a story about two good friends. Ask them to think about how these friends are alike and how they are different.

2. Read aloud "Spring" from *Frog and Toad Are Friends*. After reading the story, distribute copies of the **Character Comparison Chart (page 70)**, and place a transparency of the reproducible on the overhead. Title one bear *Frog* and the other bear *Toad*.

3. Ask students to remember details about Frog and Toad. *How does Frog feel about spring? How does Toad feel? What does Frog want to do? What does Toad want to do? What words would you use to describe Frog? To describe Toad? In what ways are Frog and Toad alike?*

4. Model how to record these ideas on the chart.

5. Divide the class into student pairs. Have each pair read another story about Frog and Toad. They can read aloud, alternating pages. Have students record new details about Frog and Toad on the chart, and then share their charts with the class.

Extended Learning
- Have students use the Character Comparison Chart to compare themselves to a friend or to a fictional character.

- Have students use their completed charts to write a brief paragraph comparing the two characters.

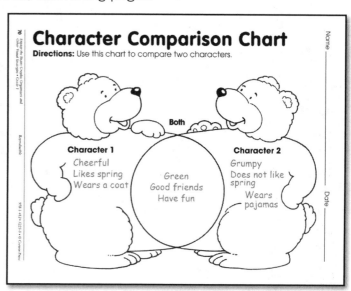

Character Comparison Chart

Directions: Use this chart to compare two characters.

Both

Character 1
Cheerful
Likes spring
Wears a coat

Green
Good friends
Have fun

Character 2
Grumpy
Does not like spring
Wears pajamas

Name

Date

Name _____ Date _____

Character Comparison Chart

Directions: Use this chart to compare two characters.

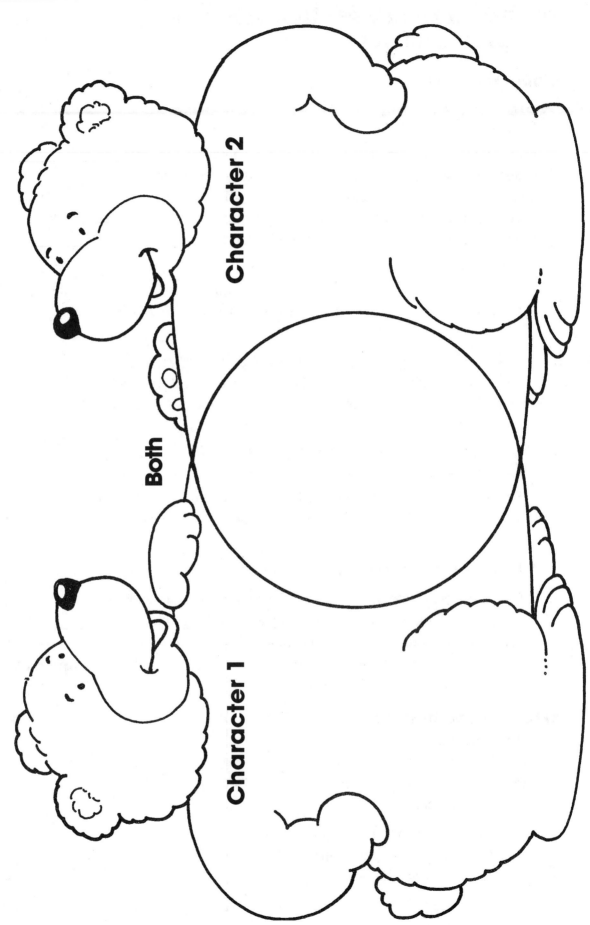

Character 2

Both

Character 1

 Engage the Brain: Graphic Organizers and Other Visual Strategies • Grade 1   Reproducible   978-1-4129-5225-5 • © Corwin Press

Homophone Match-Up: Class Book

Skills Objective

Identify and define homophones.

Materials

index cards

bag of flour

flower

drawing paper

art supplies

glue

children's picture dictionaries

Homophones are words that sound the same but have different meanings and sometimes spellings. Being able to use homophones correctly is essential for effective reading and writing. A **Class Book** presents homophones in both a textual and a visual format, making it easier for students to remember these sometimes confusing word pairs.

1. In advance, list homophones such as the following on index cards: *ant, aunt; bear, bare; be, bee; blue, blew; eye, I; flour, flower; for, four; hair, hare; hear, here; knight, night; knows, nose; pair, pear; plane, plain; sale, sail; shoe, shoo; son, sun; wear, where; one, won; week, weak.* Use one card per word.

2. Show the class a bag of flour and a flower. Ask students which item is flower/flour. Explain that both items are called flower/flour. These words are *homophones.* They sound the same but have different meanings and spellings.

3. Read the homophone cards as a class. Then mix up the cards and give one to each student. Have students circulate around the classroom and find the classmate who has the word that completes the homophone pair.

4. Have student pairs work together to make a page for a homophones book. First, they draw a line down the center of a sheet of drawing paper, dividing it in half. Then they glue each card to the bottom of the page, one on each side. Students then cut out or draw pictures to show the meaning of their words. Invite students to use picture dictionaries as references.

5. Bind all students' pages into a homophones book, and put it in the reading center. Invite students to add to the book throughout the year.

Retelling a Story: Circle Chart

Materials

Story Circle Chart
reproducible

Skills Objective

Retell story events in sequence.

Retelling the stories that students hear and read supports comprehension and helps build an understanding of story structure. A **Circle Chart** is a helpful tool for both discussing the order of story events and for composing stories.

1. Ask a volunteer to share the steps involved in getting ready for school (e.g., *I got up, ate breakfast, brushed my teeth, and walked to school*). Ask another student to retell the steps in order.

2. Point out that using a graphic organizer can make remembering and retelling story events much easier. Give students a copy of the **Story Circle Chart reproducible (page 73)**. Draw a similar chart on the board, and read the directions together.

3. Ask students to recall what happened first in the student's story. Sketch this first event of the student's day in the first quarter of the circle on the board. Continue for the second, third, and fourth events. Then have a volunteer retell the story orally, using the pictures.

4. Point out that clue words can help make the order of a story easier to understand. Model how to add words such as *first*, *next*, *then*, and *finally* to reinforce story sequence.

5. Have students use the Story Circle Chart to tell a story with illustrations. Have them write one sentence for each picture on another sheet of paper. Remind students to use clue words to indicate the order of events.

6. Pair up students with partners. Have partners tell their stories to each other. Then have them trade papers and "retell" each other's stories using the charts.

Name _____ Date _____

Story Circle Chart

Directions: Draw a picture in each part of the circle to tell a story. Write a sentence about each event.

Title: _____

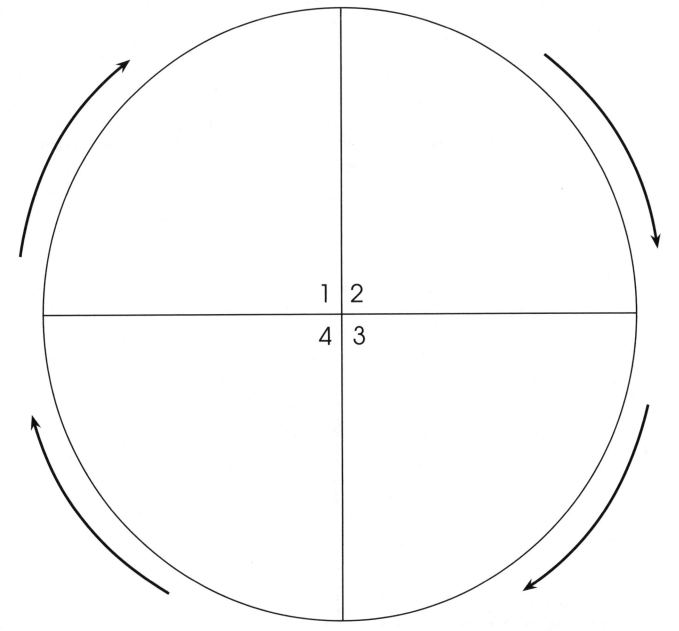

Characters Can Change: Character Map

Skills Objectives
Recall key story events.
Identify how a character changes during a story.

A **Character Map** provides a tool for students to analyze character development and story structure. By describing the character's traits at two different times during the story and comparing them, students can make keen observations about how and why a character changes.

Materials

Character Map reproducible

fairy tale

1. Read aloud a fairy tale such as *Cinderella.* Ask students to think about what the main character was like at the beginning of the story. Write *Beginning* on the board and list student responses. Write *Ending* on the board, and have students describe the character at the end of the story.

2. Discuss how Cinderella changed during the course of the story. Talk about the reasons why she changed, and write these ideas on the board.

3. On a subsequent day, share another fairy tale, such as *The Ugly Duckling*, with students. Give them a copy of the **Character Map reproducible (page 75)**, and read the directions.

4. Ask students to discuss the beginning of the story and provide words that describe the main character. Have them write these words on the first shape on the character map. Encourage students to add an illustration as well.

5. Next, have students reflect on the end of the story and describe the character at the end. Have them record how the character changed on the second shape, using words and pictures.

6. Talk about how and why the main character changed, and have students record their thoughts on their maps.

7. Close the activity by inviting students to share other characters they know from cartoons, movies, and books. Invite them to tell how a character may have changed during the story.

Character Map
Directions: Write the name of a story character. Use words and pictures to describe the character at the beginning and end of the story.

Character: The Ugly Duckling

ugly
sad
small

beautiful
happy
swan

Character at the Beginning   **Character at the End**

Character Map

Directions: Write the name of a story character. Use words and pictures to describe the character at the beginning and end of the story.

Character: _____

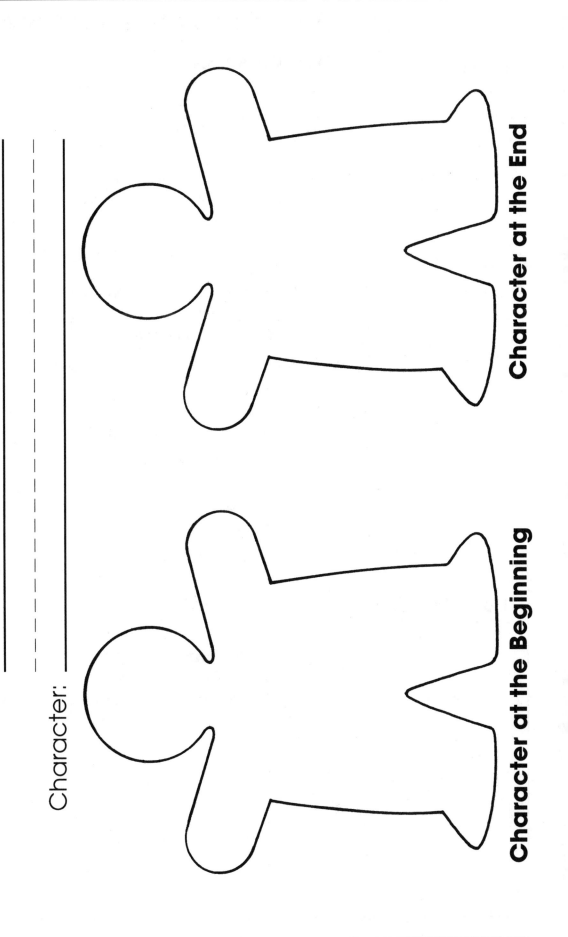

Character at the End

Character at the Beginning

Character at the End

Flowering Ideas: Brainstorming Wheel

Materials

Flowering Ideas reproducible

chart paper

Skills Objectives

Use a graphic organizer to plan writing a composition.

Brainstorm writing ideas.

Categorize ideas and topics.

In the prewriting process, students brainstorm ideas and put their thoughts on paper. A **Brainstorming Wheel** is a useful tool for generating and focusing students' thoughts on a particular topic. It can also be used as a post-reading tool for recording important ideas.

1. Ask students to share something for which they have a talent or skill. Draw a large flower shape on chart paper modeled after the **Flowering Ideas reproducible (page 77)**. Write the name of your class in the center circle (e.g., *Miss Blackburn's first-grade class*). Record student skills in one of the petals.

2. Ask students other questions about themselves, such as what they wish, what they are happy about, or what they would like to be when they grow up. Record responses in the other petals.

3. Explain that using this graphic organizer can help them think of ideas that relate to a topic or to think of writing ideas.

4. Give students a copy of the Flowering Ideas reproducible. They will use it to write ideas that relate to a topic, such as *All About Me, At the Zoo, Funny Things*, or *If I Could Fly*. Circulate among students as they work and offer guidance as needed. Remind students that they can use both words and pictures.

5. Have students use their completed papers to write or dictate a paragraph about their topic.

Extended Learning

Have students use this graphic organizer to record the main idea and details about a story they have read.

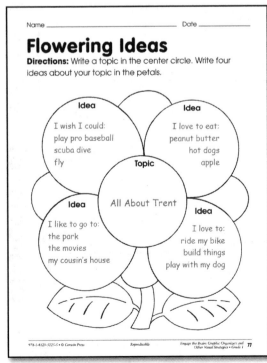

Flowering Ideas

Directions: Write a topic in the center circle. Write four ideas about your topic in the petals.

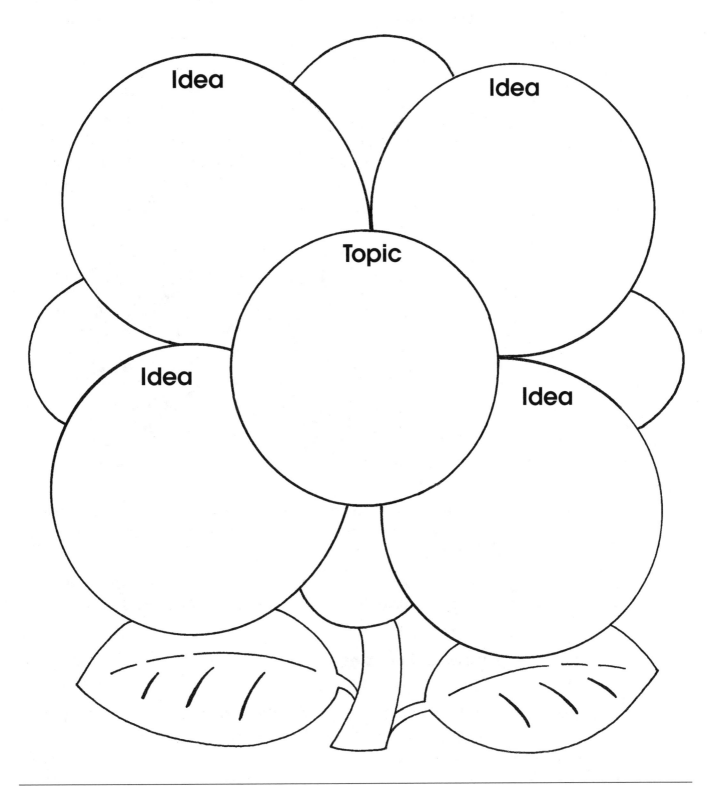

Tell Me a Story: Magazine Pictures

Materials

old magazines

scissors

glue

construction paper

Skills Objectives

Use visual prompts for oral storytelling.

Magazine Pictures make excellent visual props for learning. Parents and friends are usually happy to donate old magazines. Because cutting out pictures can be time consuming, set up an activity center in your classroom where students can look through magazines and cut out their favorite pictures. Keep pictures on hand for writing activities such as the following.

1. In advance, gather a supply of pictures. Select two or three unrelated photos and glue them to a sheet of construction paper.

2. Show the page to students and model how to make up a story that connects the photos. For example: *Once upon a time, there was a horse named Maisy. She got loose from her stable and ran away to the city. Maisy went to a bakery on the 50th floor and ate 15 pink cupcakes. Finally, she galloped home.*

3. Give each student two or three unrelated pictures for storytelling. Have students think about a story they want to tell and then glue the pictures to construction paper.

4. Ask students to tell their story to a partner. They may choose to write down the story as well. Invite volunteers to share their stories with the class.

Extended Learning

- Have students use their pictures to write illustrated stories.

- Have students glue their photos to craft sticks to make storytelling puppets. They can retell their stories using the puppets.

Build a Sentence: Pocket Chart

Skills Objectives
Identify parts of a sentence.
Compose sentences.

Materials
pocket chart

sentence strips

markers in three colors

Pocket Charts are invaluable tools that allow students to manipulate letters, words, and phrases into almost infinite combinations. In this activity, students arrange words and phrases to discover the parts of a sentence.

1. In advance, label sentence strips in three categories of phrases: *Who or What* (the subject); *Did What* (the verb); and *How or Where* (the adverb or prepositional phrase). Use a different color marker for each category. Possible phrases include:

Who or What	Did What	How or Where
A little monkey	took a nap	in a tree
My mom	ate a pie	quietly
Tia	flew	on the moon
The lion cub	swam	in a puddle
A baby	wrote a story	alone

2. Invite a small group of students to gather near the pocket chart. Show students the labels and the cards. Invite students to take turns selecting one card from each category and placing it in the chart to construct a sentence. Have students read the sentence aloud.

3. Provide a supply of blank sentence strips, and have students make their own cards for the chart. Invite them to work in small groups to construct their new sentences.

Extended Learning

- Suggest that students act out each sentence.

- Provide art supplies, and invite students to illustrate the sentences they compose.

Building Words: Magnetic Letters

Materials

magnetic letters
or alphabet cards
(or tiles)

magnet board or
metal cookie sheet

Skills Objectives

Blend sounds to make words.
Segment sounds to help spell words.
Listen for individual sounds within words.

Magnetic Letters and alphabet cards are ideal tools for visual learning. Because individual letters can be manipulated, they help students segment sounds, which is an essential skill for spelling. Students can also blend new sounds together for reading fluency. Provide each student with a set of magnetic letters or alphabet cards, or set up a learning center in which they can manipulate letters.

1. Arrange letters on a magnet board or cookie sheet so the class can see and spell a simple one-syllable word, such as *pen.* Blend the sounds and read the word together: */p/ /e/ /n/, pen.*

2. Demonstrate how to substitute a different initial letter to spell a different word (e.g., *men*). Have students segment and blend the sounds to read the new word.

3. Distribute magnetic letters or alphabet cards to students. Ask them to create the word you displayed. Then have them change one letter to make a new word. For example, if you make *men,* they can change *m* to *t* to make *ten.* Blend the sounds together as a class to check understanding.

4. After concentrating on the initial letter for a while, have students change the ending sound, and then the middle (vowel) sound, to make new words.

5. After plenty of guided practice, have students build new words with a partner, substituting one letter at a time. Have them blend the sounds and decide if the word is a real word or a nonsense word.

Extended Learning

- Introduce beginning blends using the letter manipulatives.

- Have students write sentences using several of their real words.

Photo Pals: Puppets

Skills Objective

Use puppets as props to create dialogue and tell stories.

Materials

camera

glue

heavy paper

scissors

small magnets

magnet boards or metal cookie sheets

Puppets are powerful props for oral storytelling and drama. Students enjoy experimenting with photography, and photographs make these unique puppets personal and fun! To use photography with students, get a digital camera for your classroom, or ask for donations of disposable cameras so students don't have to share.

1. Demonstrate for students how to operate a camera. Then explain that they will take pictures of their classmates and then turn the photos into puppets.

2. Have students take photos of each other. Assist them as needed. Encourage them to pose in playful and interesting poses.

3. After the photos are developed, have students glue the photos to heavy paper, cut out the figures, and glue a small magnet to the back of each.

4. Have students work in pairs or small groups to develop dialogue for their magnetic board characters. When they are satisfied with their dialogue, have them dictate it to an adult helper or teacher aide who will record the words.

5. Invite pairs or groups to share their story with the class using their puppets on a magnet board or metal cookie sheet, referring to the dictated dialogue as necessary. Encourage them to use dramatic voices to help convey the story.

CHAPTER 5

Physical Education, Art, and Music

My Fitness Goals: Goal-Setting Chart

Materials

My Fitness Goals reproducible

chart paper

Skills Objectives

Set goals for physical fitness.
Work toward completing fitness goals.

Students take pride in the things their growing bodies can do. A **Goal-Setting Chart** helps them document and celebrate their physical accomplishments. As you explore this activity with students, be sure to help them set realistic goals and focus on their personal success.

1. Discuss with students all the ways their bodies can move. Ask them to brainstorm things their bodies can do. Record their ideas on chart paper.

2. Review the list together. Have students reflect on the things they already know how to do and those they would like to learn to do.

3. Ask students to describe the word *goal*. Point out that this word has multiple meanings. A goal can be the end of a race or part of a game. A goal can also be something people want to earn or achieve.

4. Talk about the steps in setting a goal. Point out that a goal should be realistic. When people set a goal, they often set a deadline or date by which they will accomplish that goal.

5. Give students a copy of the **My Fitness Goals reproducible (page 83)**. Read the directions together. Review the class list, and have each student choose three things they know how to do and one thing they want to learn.

6. As students work, take time to discuss their goals with them. Have students review their charts occasionally. Recognize and celebrate their accomplishments, and encourage them to set new fitness goals throughout the year.

My Fitness Goals

Directions: Write three things you know how to do. Write a goal for one thing you want to learn to do.

Things I Can Do

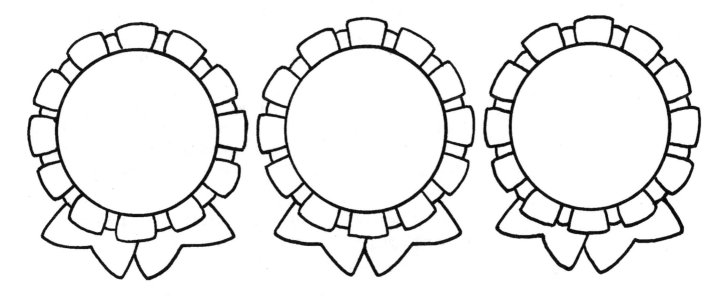

My Goal

Color Recipe: Color Chart

<table>
<tr><td valign="top">

Materials

Color Chart
reproducible

tempera paint in
primary colors

paintbrushes

cups of water

paper towels

</td><td valign="top">

Skills Objectives

Mix primary colors.
Identify secondary colors.

Mixing paint colors and recording these combinations on a **Color Chart** provides students with hands-on exploration and valuable practice in color theory. The finished chart provides a useful reference for future art activities.

1. Ask students if they know which colors can be mixed together to make all other colors. *(red, yellow, blue)* These three colors are called *primary colors.* Explain that students will get to mix primary colors to make *secondary colors.*

2. Invite students to watch as you mix red paint with blue paint. Ask them to predict what color will result. *(purple)* Ask students: *How can I remember what color these two colors make?* Lead them to understand that a color chart is a tool for recording color combinations.

3. Demonstrate how to record this combination on the **Color Chart reproducible (page 85)**. Ask students which colors on your paper are primary *(red and blue)*, and which is secondary *(purple)*.

4. Provide students with paint and their own copy of the Color Chart. Invite them to combine the colors and record the results. For the last entry, they may mix any two colors (even secondary colors) to make a new color. Remind them to use a clean brush when using each new color and to trace over the color words.

</td></tr>
</table>

Extended Learning

- Give students sample paint colors, and have them try to match the colors.

- Have students make up interesting, fun names for the colors they mix.

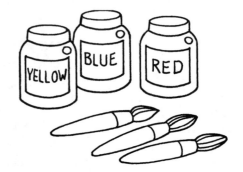

Color Chart

Directions: Trace the color words. Add the correct color paint above each word. Mix the two colors. Show the new color and write the color word.

red + blue = purple

blue + yellow = green

yellow + red = orange

red + white = pink

Name

Date

Name _____ Date _____

Color Chart

Directions: Trace the color words. Add the correct color paint above each word. Mix the two colors. Show the new color and write the color word.

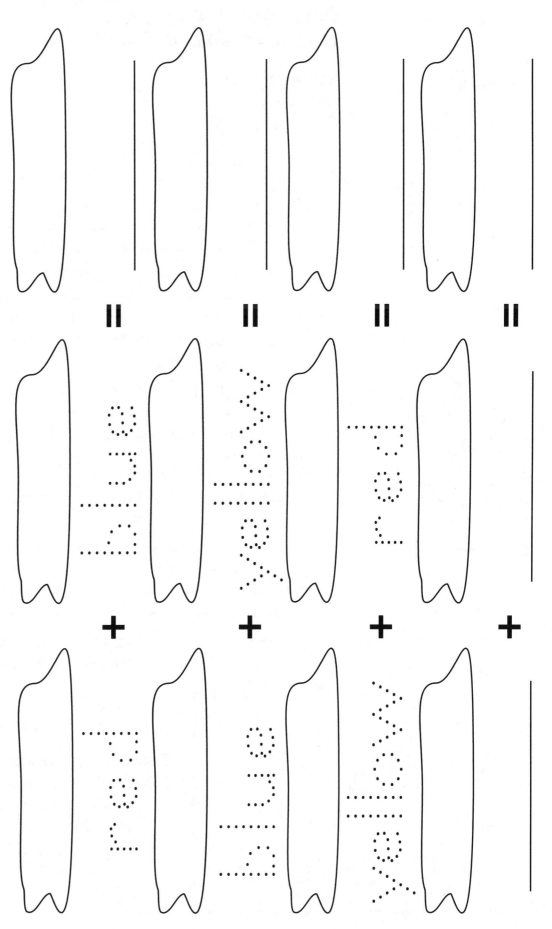

Draw What You See: Line and Shape Chart

Materials

I Can Draw!
reproducible

drawing paper

black felt-tip markers

Skills Objectives

Make careful observations.
Utilize lines and shapes to draw.

Lines and shapes are fundamental elements of art. A **Line and Shape Chart** helps students to observe before they draw.

1. Distribute drawing paper to students. Have them fold the paper so there are four sections. Tell students to draw a box in one section and a birthday cake in another. Ask: *How did you do?* Explain that you will show them a trick to draw objects even better.

2. Explain that all drawings are made of lines and shapes. We must train our eyes to look closely at the lines and shapes to draw objects as they really are. Tell students they will redraw the two objects along with you.

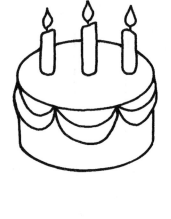

3. Read aloud the following directions as you draw, while students follow along: *To make a box, draw a diamond shape. Draw a straight line coming down from the left and right corners of the diamond. Draw a little longer line down from the bottom corner. Connect the ends of the three lines.* Walk around the room to see if students were able to follow your instructions.

4. Continue with the cake: *To make a cake, draw an oval on its side. Draw two straight lines coming down from each end. Connect the ends of the lines with a curved line. Add a few candles on top.* Again, check that students followed your instructions. Have students compare their original drawings with their new ones.

5. Distribute the **I Can Draw! reproducible (page 87)**. Have students look at each picture and copy one line or shape at a time in the box below and then trace finished drawings with black marker.

Extended Learning

Create new designs on the I Can Draw! reproducible so students can practice copying lines and shapes.

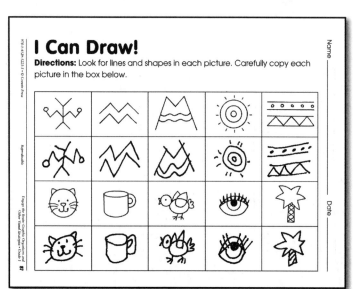

Name _____ Date _____

I Can Draw!

Directions: Look for lines and shapes in each picture. Carefully copy each picture in the box below.

Self-Portrait: Face Model

Materials

Face Model
reproducible

small mirrors

drawing paper

pencils, crayons,
markers

Skills Objectives

Observe facial features to create self-portraits.
Use guidelines to draw proportionately.

A self-portrait can begin with a basic egg shape sitting on a smaller tube-shaped neck. A **Face Model** helps students by giving them the guidelines of shape and the positioning of facial features so their own self-portraits and portraits of others are more accurate and lifelike.

1. Ask students to help you draw a self-portrait on the board. (Do not worry about your own inadequacies as an artist; students will be inspired by your efforts!) Use a mirror each time you draw something to model for students how you must look carefully first at what you want to draw.

2. Ask students what shape your head is. Many may say a *circle*, but ask them to look more carefully to see that it is more of an oval, or egg shape. Place your head on a vertical line for a neck. Ask if that looks right. It looks like the head will tip over, so erase it and draw a tube-shaped neck, so it can support your head. Ask a volunteer to tell where to put your eyes. While the student may suggest placing them at the top of the shape, eyes are actually in the middle of the head.

3. Give students a copy of the **Face Model reproducible (page 89)**, along with small mirrors and drawing paper. Remind them to draw lightly with pencil until everything is in place. Have students look in their mirror and begin their self-portrait by drawing their head and neck shapes. Have them refer to the Face Model for guidelines as to where their facial features should be placed.

4. Check that students are using their mirrors to look closely at their face and not just drawing circles for eyes and a curved line for a mouth. Once students have their features in place, they may add color or leave it as a sketch. Display self-portraits around the room to create a class portrait gallery!

Name _____   Date _____

Face Model

Directions: Use this model to help draw your self-portrait.

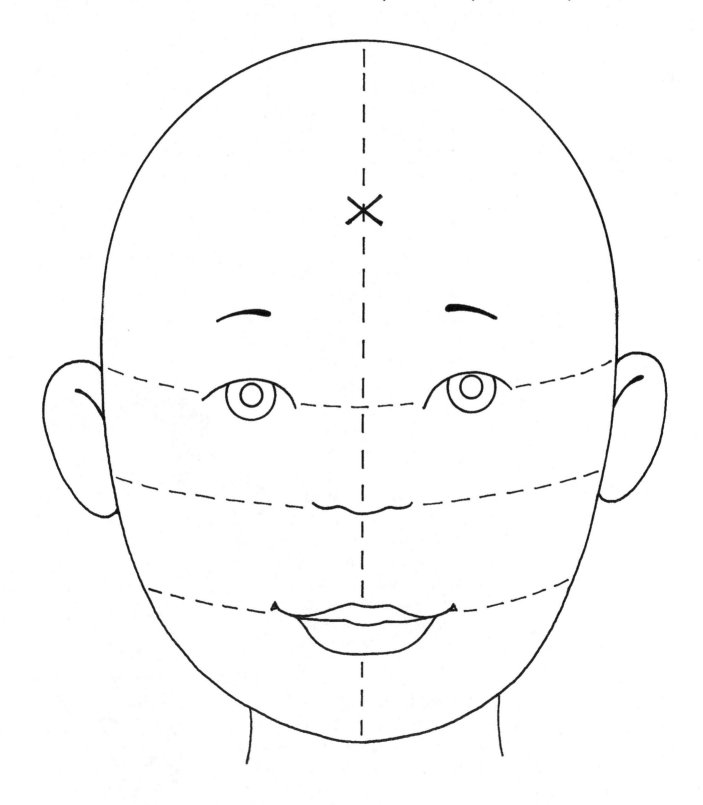

Dance Me a Feeling! Feelings Chart

Materials

Feelings Faces reproducible

variety of music CDs or audiocassettes

CD or cassette player

overhead projector

transparency

Skills Objective

Interpret feelings through dance.

Dance offers students a creative outlet for emotional expression. A **Feelings Chart** provides visual prompts, making it easier for students to access and express their feelings. In this activity, students interpret picture cues through dance.

1. Talk to students about the reasons people dance. Guide them to understand that dancing is a way of telling stories and expressing feelings. Dancers use their faces and bodies to show feelings. Tell students that they will have the opportunity to express feelings through dance.

2. Ask students to use their body and face to show what "happy" looks like.

3. Display a transparency of the **Feelings Faces reproducible (page 91)** on the overhead. Discuss the emotion expressed by each face and when students might have felt that emotion. Then point to one of the faces, play some appropriate music, and ask students to express that emotion through dance. Continue with each of the emotions on the page.

4. Let students take turns choosing a face for the rest of the class to interpret through dance. At the end of the activity, discuss with students their favorite, easiest, and most difficult emotions to express through dance. Prompt them with questions such as: *Were you scared when you danced for the scared face? What did you think about? Did you think about things that scare you?*

Extended Learning

Play music and have students point to the face on the Feelings Faces Chart that best shows how the music makes them feel.

Feeling Faces

Fast or Slow? Tempo Chart

Materials

Tempo Chart reproducible

variety of music CDs or audiotapes

CD or cassette player

Skills Objectives

Identify tempo.
Sing and move to different tempos.

Presenting musical concepts in a chart, such as a **Tempo Chart**, helps students form a connection between what they see and hear. Make charts for the songs students enjoy singing, and use visual tools such as the following tempo chart.

1. Sing a favorite song with students, such as "Down by the Bay." Begin by singing the song at the regular tempo. Sing the song again, this time slightly faster. Then sing it faster still, as if driving in a race car.

2. Explain to students that the speed of music is called *tempo*. Point out that tempo can be fast, medium, or slow. Sing the song again, this time very slowly.

3. When students can identify different tempos, distribute the **Tempo Chart reproducible (page 93)**. Point to a line on the chart, and have students sing and move in the corresponding tempo. Repeat several times.

4. Later, play different selections of music for students. Invite them to decide which tempo best matches each piece.

Extended Learning

Teach students different musical terms, such as *adagio* (slow), *moderato* (medium), *allegro* (fast), *tenor*, *bass*, *alto*, and *soprano*.

Tempo Chart

Very Fast	
Fast	
Medium	
Slow	
Very Slow	

Singing and Signing: ASL Alphabet Chart

Materials

ASL Alphabet Chart reproducible

overhead projector

transparency

Skills Objectives

Interpret and use ASL signs for alphabet letters.
Use hand signs while singing.

American Sign Language is not just for the hearing impaired. With the addition of hand signs, singing familiar songs can become newly enriching experiences. An **ASL Alphabet Chart** will help students communicate in a new language they will remember longer when put to music. Learn a few ASL signs to share with students throughout the year, and watch their ability to communicate grow.

1. Ask students: *How can you talk without making a sound?* Encourage them to share their ideas, and then lead them to understand that sign language is one way of communicating without sound. Explain that people who are hearing impaired use sign language to talk with each other.

2. Tell students that they are going to learn a new way of singing a song they already know.

3. Place a transparency of the **ASL Alphabet Chart (page 95)** on the overhead. Read the alphabet letters together, and model how to form the sign for *A*. Have students imitate the sign.

4. On subsequent days, review the signs you have learned, and practice one or two new signs.

5. Once students have learned the first few signs, put these signs to music. Sing the alphabet song with the addition of ASL signs.

6. When students have mastered all 26 signs, send home a copy of the ASL Alphabet Chart, and encourage them to teach the song to their families.

Extended Learning

- Invest in a book of ASL signs and teach students to sign key words and phrases in other favorite songs.

- Use the ASL Alphabet Chart to make flashcards for classroom learning centers.

Name _____   Date _____

ASL Alphabet Chart

A	B	C	D	E	F
G	H	I	J	K	L
M	N	O	P	Q	R
S	T	U	V	W	X
Y	Z				

References

The Anne Frank Center USA Online. (n.d.). *Timeline*. Retrieved August 30, 2006, from http://www.annefrank.com/2_life_timeline_5.htm.

Bromley, K., Irwin-De Vitis, L., & Modlo, M. (1995). *Graphic organizers: Visual strategies for active learning*. New York, NY: Scholastic Professional Books.

Civardi, A., & Cartwright, S. (1985). *Things people do*. London, England: Usborne Publishing.

Edom, H. (2006). *Why do tigers have stripes?* London, England: Usborne Publishing.

Gardner, H. (1983). *Frames of mind: The theory of multiple intelligences*. New York, NY: Basic Books.

Hall, T., & Strangman, N. (2002). *Graphic organizers*. Retrieved August 15, 2006, from the CAST Universal Design for Learning Web site: www.cast.org/publications/ncac/ncac_go.html.

Henkes, K. (2000). *Wemberly worried*. New York, NY: Greenwillow.

Hyerle, D. (1996). *Visual tools for constructing knowledge*. Alexandria, VA: Association for Supervision and Curriculum Development (ASCD).

Jensen, E., & Johnson, G. (1994). *The learning brain*. San Diego, CA: Turning Point for Teachers.

Kalman, B. (2001). *What are camouflage and mimicry?* New York, NY: Crabtree Books.

Lobel, A. (1970). *Frog and Toad are friends*. New York, NY: HarperCollins.

McCarthy, B. (1990). Using the 4MAT system to bring learning styles to schools. *Educational Leadership, 48*(2), 31–37.

Morris, A. (1995). *Houses and homes*. New York, NY: HarperTrophy.

National Council for the Social Studies. (2002). *Expectations of excellence: Curriculum standards for social studies*. Silver Spring, MD: National Council for the Social Studies (NCSS).

National Council of Teachers of English and International Reading Association. (1996). *Standards for the English language arts*. Urbana, IL: National Council of Teachers of English (NCTE).

National Council of Teachers of Mathematics. (2005). *Principles and standards for school mathematics*. Reston, VA: National Council of Teachers of Mathematics (NCTM).

National Research Council. (2005). *National science education standards*. Washington, DC: National Academy Press.

Ogle, D. M. (2000). Make it visual: A picture is worth a thousand words. In M. McLaughlin & M. Vogt (Eds.), *Creativity and innovation in content area teaching*. Norwood, MA: Christopher-Gordon.

Pohl, K. (2005). *What happens at a toy factory?* Stanford, CT: Weekly Reader Books.

Selsam, M. P. (1992). *How kittens grow*. New York, NY: Cartwheel.

Steig, W. (1998). *Pete's a pizza*. New York, NY: HarperCollins.

Sweeney, J. (1999). *Me and my place in space*. New York, NY: Dragonfly.

Tate, M. L. (2003). *Worksheets don't grow dendrites: 20 instructional strategies that engage the brain*. Thousand Oaks, CA: Corwin Press.